The Book of
Kitchen
WITCHERY

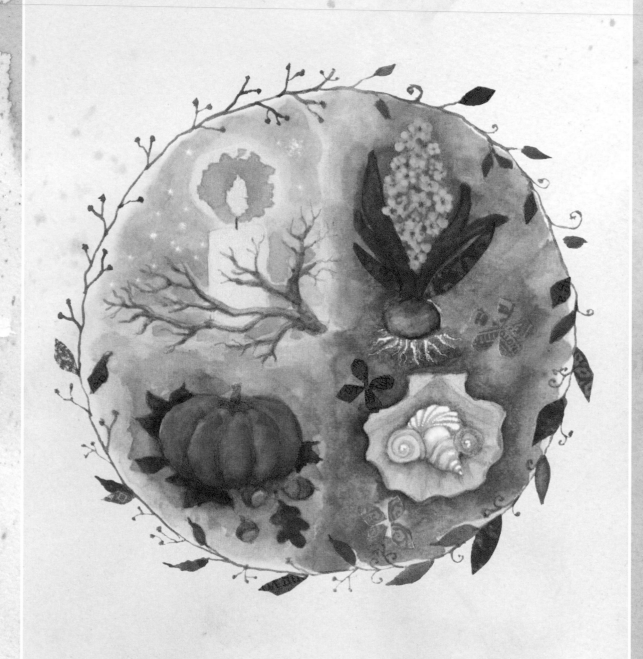

The Book of
Kitchen
WITCHERY

Spells, recipes, and rituals for magical meals,
an enchanted garden, and a happy home

Cerridwen Greenleaf

CICO BOOKS
LONDON NEW YORK

To Z Budapest who taught me so much about the path: eternal love for your huge heart and brilliant mind.
"We all come from the goddess and to her we shall return, like a drop of water, flowing to the ocean."

Published in 2016 by CICO Books
An imprint of Ryland Peters & Small Ltd
20–21 Jockey's Fields   341 E 116th St
London WC1R 4BW   New York, NY 10029

www.rylandpeters.com

10

Text © Brenda Knight 2016
Design and illustration © CICO Books 2016

A CIP catalog record for this book is available from the Library of Congress and the British Library.

ISBN: 978-1-78249-372-3

Printed in China

Editor: Jennifer Jahn
Designer: Emily Breen
Illustrator: Emma Garner

Commissioning editor: Kristine Pidkameny
Senior editor: Carmel Edmonds
Art director: Sally Powell
Production manager: Gordana Simakovic
Publishing manager: Penny Craig
Publisher: Cindy Richards

FSC
www.fsc.org

MIX
Paper from
responsible sources
FSC® C106563

Contents

Introduction:
The Charmed Life

No matter how humble, kitchens are where we gather together. The very stuff of life takes place in this room—cooking, sharing meals, and talking about our lives. What can be more sacred than this? Nothing. For pagans, far more than meals are prepared in this space. All manner of concoctions and cures are created here. Herbs are ground up, blends are brewed, essential oils are bottled, healing teas are steeped, tinctures are carefully measured—to name but a few of the duties of the kitchen witch.

The kitchen of a witch is a thing to behold—a sacred space where good health, prosperity, and love can be conjured. The kitchen is truly the heart of the home, imbued with positive energy. Magic and spellwork are about expansion—expanding your horizons, enriching your mind and spirit, and celebrating the real riches of well-being and contentment. Every witch walks the spiritual path with practical feet, navigating the modern world aided by ancient wisdom, handed down generation after generation. When you begin to access this special kind of knowledge, you join a lineage of folks who are more in tune with the natural world around us—our Mother Earth, the moon and the stars, herbs and plants, animal allies. All these are nature's gifts and you will use them in the sanctity of your kitchen. As soon

as you approach your magic consciously, you will see that you have the power to choose abundance. Then you can move on to the truest kind of prosperity, which has nothing to do with material gains, but involves sharing blessings with loved ones and your community. It is creating meaning and happy memories.

Magic resides inside of us; we create it with our thoughts and actions. It is our deepest power and we are all born with it. The goal of ritual is to bring about needed change. It is how we make things better for ourselves, for our friends and loved ones, and for our community and our world. You are not just sipping a homemade healing tea in your cozy kitchen, you are performing a ritual like many before you. This book is designed with you in mind, to encourage and empower you to live life to the fullest and, most importantly, to access the wisdom that comes so naturally to you. With just a few of the ideas in this compendium of inspiration, you'll soon be brewing potent potions from your own herb garden, crafting auspicious altars, fermenting supernatural spirits in your pantry, serving feasts to the people you love in honor of seasonal festivals, and engaging in highly satisfying spellwork. Summon the power of domestic gods and goddesses at your disposal and, above all, relish every joy-filled day of this gift called life.

Chapter 1

The Kitchen Altar

Your personal altar is the ideal place to incubate your ideas, your hopes, and your intentions. It can become a touchstone for morning blessings and simple daily rituals. As you evolve, so will your altar. It will become an outward expression of your inner life and your spiritual growth, inspiring you to commune with the deepest parts of yourself. An altar is a where you honor the rhythms of the season as well as the rhythms of your own life. Your altar is a center for enchantment in your home, where you connect with the sacred each and every day. Creating and augmenting your holy shrine is one of the most self-nurturing acts you can perform. When mind, body, and spirit align, there is nothing more magical.

Your Personal Power Center

Before there were temples and churches, the primary place for expressing reverence was the altar. The word "altar" comes from the Latin, meaning "high." With a personal altar, you can reach the heights of your spiritual ascension in wisdom. You construct an altar when you assemble symbolic items in a meaningful manner and focus both your attention and your intention. When you work with the combined energies of these items, you are performing a ritual. Your rituals can arise from your needs, imagination, or the seasonal and traditional ceremonies that you find in this book and others. A book from which I draw much inspiration has been Nancy Brady Cunningham's *A Book of Women's Altars*, and I love her advice to bow or place your hands on the ground in front of your altar at the beginning of ritual work and at the closing. She explains that "Grounding symbolizes the end of the ritual and signals to the mind to return to an ordinary state of awareness as you re-enter daily life." An altar is a physical point of focus for the ritual, containing items considered sacred and essential to ritual work and spiritual growth. An altar can be anything from a rock in the forest to an exquisitely carved antique table. Even portable or temporary altars can suffice, such as a board suspended between two chairs for "rituals on the go."

Creating Your Kitchen Altar

On a low table or chest of your choosing, place a forest-green cloth and a brown candle to represent family and home. Add lovely objects you have gathered, including items from the garden and the outdoors: ocean-carved driftwood, a gorgeous flower, a dried seedpod, a favorite crystal—whatever pleases your eye. It is of the utmost importance to add a bouquet of wildflowers native to your area, which you should have gathered close to where you live or bought locally. These posies will help integrate you and your home into your neighborhood and geographic region. Add a sweetly scented sachet of herbs from your kitchen garden or those you intend to plant—for example, rosemary, lavender, thyme, or mint, all of which imbue your space with positive energy. Burn associated essential oils, choosing those which will create an aura of comfort around your kitchen, including vanilla, cinnamon, or sweet-orange neroli in an oil lamp. Finally, anoint the brown candle, concentrating on the power of peace and bliss surrounding your home and all around your kitchen altar. Chant the words below:

Peace and plenty are in abundance
And here true bliss surrounds,
From now on, all disharmony is gone,
This is a place of powerful blessings
For here lives sheer joy.
And so it is—blessed be!

This consecrated space will ease your spirits at any time. Your altar connects you to the earth of which you are a part.

Sanctuary Spell

To anoint your home and turn it into a protective shield for you and your loved ones, rub any of the following essential oils on your doorjambs—cinnamon, clove, dragon's blood, myrrh. Walk through the door into your home and close it securely. Take the remaining essential oils and rub a bit on all other doors and windows. Light anointed white candles and place them in the windows and chant the words of the spell on the right.

My home is my temple.
Here I live and love,
Safe and secure,
Both below and above.
And so it is by magic sealed.

Kitchen Magic Altar Herbs

* **Cinnamon** refreshes and directs spirituality; it is a protection herb and handy for healing, money, love, sensuality, personal power, and success with work and creative projects.

* **Clove** is good for bringing money to you and for helping evade negative energies and block them.

* **Lavender** is a potent healer that calms and aids deep rest and dreams.

* **Myrrh** has been considered to be very sacred since ancient times and will intensify your spirituality. It also wards off bad spirits.

* **Nutmeg** is a lucky herb that promotes good health and abundance. It also encourages loyalty and marital fidelity.

* **Peppermint** is an herb of purification and increases psychic powers. Mint brings relaxation and can help you sleep, reducing anxiety.

* **Rosemary** purifies and increases memory and intelligence. This savory plant also heightens sensuality and bonds of love. It will also keep you youthful!

* **Sage** brings wisdom, health, and a long life. It is very useful for dispelling negative vibrations and encouraging cleansing. Sage can help your wishes come true, too.

* **Star anise** aids divination and psychic abilities.

* **Tonka bean** will give you courage and draws love and money.

* **Vanilla** is an herb of love and expands and enriches your mental capacity.

Pot of Gold: Abundance Altar Blessing

Cauldron magic is more about the acts of brewing something new than it is about purification by water. To attract money, fill a big pot with fresh water and place it on your altar during the waxing moon. Pour a cup of milk with a tablespoon of honey and a tablespoon of ground cloves into the pot as an offering. Toss handfuls of dried chamomile, moss, and vervain into the vessel. With your head raised high, say aloud:

I call upon you, gods and goddesses of old, to fill my purse with gold.
I offer you mother's milk and honey sweet.
With harm to none and blessings to thee, I honor you for bringing me
health and prosperity.

Place the offering bowl on your altar and leave the aromatic mixture there to instill your kitchen with the energy of abundance. After four hours and forty-four minutes, go outside your home and pour the offering into your kitchen garden or into the roots of a shrub. Then bow in appreciation of the kindness of the gods and goddesses.

FLORAL FUNDING

The following list of plants can be used in any ritual work whose intention is prosperity: allspice, almond, basil, bergamot, cedar leaves, cinnamon, cinquefoil, clover, dill, ginger, heliotrope, honeysuckle, hyssop, jasmine, mint, myrtle, nutmeg, oak moss, sassafras, vervain, and woodruff. Try these alone or in mixtures, tinctures, or grind into your incenses. You can also plant a prosperity garden and refresh your abundance altar with herbs and flowers grown by your own hand.

Salt of the Earth Blessing Spell

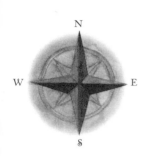

Every kitchen has a box of salt. This most common of seasonings is essential to physical health and also to the health of your home. With a bowl of salt alone, you can purify your home every day and have a "safe zone" for ritual work. You can leave a bowl of pure salt in any room you feel is in need of freshening; the salt absorbs negativity. Many a kitchen witch uses this homely approach on a daily basis early in the day, tidying up and cleansing energy to charge the home with positivity.

In your kitchen, take a bowl of water, freshly drawn, and a small cup of salt. Take the vessel of water and sprinkle in as much salt as you feel is needed. Anoint your fingers by dipping them in the salt water and then touch your forehead around your third eye in the middle of your forehead.

Now turn to the east and say:

Power of the East,
Source of the Sun rising,
Bring me new beginnings.

After speaking, sprinkle some of the water in the eastern part of your kitchen.

Face south and say:

Source of the Starry Cross,
Place of warmth and light,
Bring me joy and bounty.

Scatter droplets of salt water in the southern direction.

Face the west and speak aloud:

Powers of the West,
Source of oceans, mountains,
and deserts all,
Bring me the security of the ground
beneath my feet.

Scatter droplets of water in the west side of your kitchen.

Face north now and speak aloud:

Powers of the North,
Bringer of winds and the polestar,
Show me vision and insight.

Sprinkle water in the northern area of the room.

End this ritual by sprinkling water and salt all around your home, especially around windows, sills, doorways, and thresholds where energy passes in and out as visitors and delivery people come and go. In this way, you are cleansing and managing the energy of your space. After a distressing occurrence, you can repeat this ritual and then leave a bowl of salt out for 24 hours so it can rid your sacred space of negative "vibes."

Kitchen Warming Spell

When you or a friend move into a new home, place a wreath on the front door and also on the outside of the kitchen or back door (if your kitchen doesn't lead directly outside). Gather two bundles of dried hops or eucalyptus, tie them with green and brown ribbons, and hang them high on the door. Walk through each door with a brown candle in a glass votive jar and aromatic cinnamon incense. Intone these words:

House of my body, I accept your shelter.
Home of my heart, I receive your blessings.
Home of my heart, I am open to joy.
And so it is. And so it shall be.

All the Seasons and Reasons for Altars

One of the most vital ways pagans can keep in touch with nature is through the creation of seasonal altars. Your altar helps you to maintain balance in your life and deepen your spiritual connection to the world around you. A seasonal altar is your tool for ceremonies to honor Mother Nature and receive the deep wisdom of the earth by blending the energies of shells, feathers, leaves, flowers, herbs, and all of the gifts of the season. Your periodic altars are the middle ground between Earth and sky, the meeting point of the four elements. Creating these altars is very life-affirming.

Spring

You can create a wonderful outdoor altar for spring by planning two seasons ahead and planting floral bulbs—flowers that are the very harbingers of spring such as tulips and lilies of the valley. When the bulbs begin to grow and bud, place an image or statue in the center of your altar, which could be a stone bench or the top of a rock wall. It could be a bust of a mythological youth to represent Hyacinth, immortalized in myth and in the gorgeous flower itself. Throughout the spring, you can stand inside your magic circle (see page 25) and pray and chant for the rebirth of nature that is spring.

Summer

During the season of sun and heat, the fullness of life and growth can be celebrated with the colors of yellow, green, and red. As you go on vacation, bring back shells and stones and create an altar devoted to this season of joy. As a card-carrying hearth witch, I have an outdoor fireplace, which is my seasonal shrine, and I adorn it with a lei of orchids, a spell bottle filled with sparkly golden sand, and gleaming shells from the beach. A yellow votive candle placed in a gorgeous opalescent abalone shell gently flames. An old brick imprinted with an image of the sun sits upright, standing guard over the humble shrine to the season of Helios.

Fall

Bring the bounty of the harvest to your kitchen altar. The leaves are falling and reaping-time is here. Now is the time for a gratitude altar reflecting the bounty and continuity of life. An arrangement of pumpkins, acorns, multicolored branches, and a handsome wreath will honor this time of abundance.

Winter

White and blue represent snow and sky. Star-shaped candles and a bare branch on your altar symbolize this time to go within, explore the inner reaches of self, and draw forth the insight for the coming spring. If you have a fireplace inside, this can be your altar for the coldest season, with candles burning to help create comfort and warmth.

Witching Hour Altar for Well-Being

Creating a health altar will safeguard your physical health and that of your loved ones. Your altar is a sacred workspace and, in this case, a place of potent and practical magic. Set up your healing altar facing north, the direction associated with the energy of manifestation. North is also the direction of the midnight hour, sometimes known as the "Witching Hour."

Find a pure white square of fabric to drape over your altar for clean and clear new beginnings. Take two green candles and place them in green glass holders and position them in the two farthest corners. Place your censer in between and burn sandalwood, camphor, or frankincense for purification. Adorn your altar with objects that connote well-being to you. Perhaps an amethyst candleholder with purple candles, a bowl of bright red apples from your backyard, a dwarf lemon tree bursting with the restorative power of Vitamin C, a crock of curative salts from the sea. These symbolic items and any others you select will imbue your altar with the magic that lives inside of you and your intention toward good health. It is imperative that the altar be pleasing to your eye and fill you with gladness when you gaze upon it. After you have been performing midnight-hour rituals there for a while, a positive healing energy field will radiate from your altar. Blessed be!

Astrological Almanac of Green Witchery

Plants carry potent energy you can use to amplify your magical workings. Use the signs of the Sun, Moon, and stars to your advantage and, over time, you will come to know which ones are most effective for you. Make sure to use your own astrological chart in working with these herbs.

Here is a guide to the astrological associations of plants you may be growing in your kitchen garden or keep dried in your pantry:

* **Aries**, ruled by Mars: carnation, cedar wood, clove, cumin, fennel, juniper, peppermint, and pine

* **Taurus**, ruled by Venus: apple, daisy, lilac, magnolia, oak moss, orchid, plumeria (frangipani), rose, thyme, tonka bean, vanilla, and violet

* **Gemini**, ruled by Mercury: almond, bergamot, clover, dill, lavender, lemongrass, lily, mint, and parsley

* **Cancer**, ruled by the Moon: eucalyptus, gardenia, jasmine, lemon, lotus, myrrh, rose, and sandalwood

* **Leo**, ruled by the Sun: acacia, cinnamon, heliotrope, nutmeg, orange, and rosemary

* **Virgo**, ruled by Mercury: almond, cypress, bergamot, mace, mint, moss, patchouli, and thyme

* **Libra**, ruled by Venus: catnip, marjoram, mugwort, spearmint, sweet pea, thyme, and vanilla

* **Scorpio**, ruled by Pluto: allspice, basil, cumin, galangal, and ginger

* **Sagittarius**, ruled by Jupiter: anise, cedar wood, honeysuckle, sassafras, and star anise

* **Capricorn**, ruled by Saturn: lemon thyme, mimosa, vervain, and vetiver

* **Aquarius**, ruled by Uranus: citron, cypress, gum, lavender, pine, and spearmint

* **Pisces**, ruled by Neptune: clover, neroli, orris, sarsaparilla, and sweet pea

Power Potpourri

¼ cup (5g) dried rosemary

4 dried bay laurel leaves

⅛ cup (5g) dried sage

1 teaspoon dried juniper berries

Simmer this mixture in a pot of water on your stove whenever you feel the need to infuse your space with protection or want an energetic turnaround from negative to positive. A bad day at work, family squabble, an unfortunate incident in your neighborhood: instead of just muddling along, you can do something about it, and your creation of the positive will help you and your loved ones as well as your neighbors. This power potpourri will also safeguard you from outside influences that can be disruptive. Set your intention before gathering the herbs from your stores.

Mix the herbs together by hand. While you are sifting them through your fingers, close your eyes and visualize your home protected by a boundary of glowing white light. Imagine the light running through you to the herbs in your hand and charging them with the energy of safety, sanctity, and protection. Add the herbs to slowly simmering water and breathe in the newly charged air.

Stone Altar Spell—Burning Away Bad Luck

Your kitchen is the heart of your home, your sanctuary. Yet the world is constantly coming in and bringing mundane energy over your threshold—problems at the workplace, financial woes, bad news from your neighborhood or the world at large. All this negativity wants to get in the way and stay. While you can't do anything about the stock market crash in China or a co-worker's divorce, you can do something about not allowing this bad energy to cling to you by using this home-keeping spell. The best times to release any and all bad luck are on a Friday 13th or on any waxing moon. As you know, Friday 13th is considered a lucky day on the witch's calendar.

Get a big black candle and a black crystal, a piece of white paper, a black pen with black ink, and a cancellation stamp, readily available at any stationery store. Go into your backyard or a nearby park or woodlands and find a flat rock that has a slightly concave surface. Using the pen, write down on the white paper that of which you want to rid yourself and your home; this is your release request. Place the candle and the black crystal on the rock; light the candle, and while it burns, intone the words of the spell on the right.

Waxing moon, most wise Selene,
From me this burden please dispel
Upon this night so clear and bright
I release ___ to the moon tonight.

Visualize a clear and peaceful home filled with only positivity as the candle burns for 13 minutes. Stamp the paper with the cancel stamp. Snuff the candle, fold the paper away from your body, and place it under the rock. Speak your thanks to the moon for assisting you. If you have a truly serious issue at hand, repeat the process for 13 nights and all will be vanquished.

Coming Full Circle

"The more use an altar gets, the more energy it builds up, making your spells even more effective and powerful."

Chapter 2

Tools of the Trade

Your tools collect and hold the magic that lives inside of you. They will become instilled with your energy and become a source of power for you and magnify the strength of your ritual work. Additional tools at your disposal are less tangible than knives, cauldrons, herbs, and wands; these are your breath, visualization, your intuition, an ability to focus your thoughts and emotions. Your intention purifies all these additional skills in your arsenal. As you walk the path of a sacred life, know that everything you do can be a vessel to carry enchantment: each seed you plant, every tea you brew, every meal you prepare for your loved ones. There is great joy in this along with great responsibility. With this special mix of positive and practical magic, kitchen witchery can be your means to bring much good to the world.

Your Magical Space

Kitchens have many more tools that most workshops. Modern kitchens are filled with the latest gadgets along with the tried and true tools that humans have been using for thousands of years, since the first caveman sharpened a stick into a meat skewer and the first cavewoman started using shells for spoons and bowls. These primordial implements sustained life as the first humans used them to cook by the tribal fire. That which has been used from the beginning—kitchen tools forged by fire and used for survival against the elements—is part of the lineage of hearth witches, which informs the life of the twenty-first century kitchen witch.

While we need not struggle against the harshness of early life, our forebears forged a different kind of relationship with the elements of Earth, Air, Fire, and Water. We now harness these energies in spellwork and tap into the power and good therein: bowls carved from earthen clay, cups and chalices pouring sacred waters, the heat of the flame for cooking, and the scented, magical, smoky air of the censer filled with resins and herbs. These simple acts connect us to our ancestors and to our future sons and daughters.

A Magic Circle

When you create a sacred space and use your magical tools in it, you are leaving behind the mundane. Your kitchen is a space where you will make much magic and, despite the hurly-burly of the daily world around us, you can touch the sacrosanct. There is no need to ascend to the top of a holy mountain; anywhere you choose can be an arena of enchantment where you cast the circle.

The magic circle is created by "casting," or drawing in the air with concentrated energy. Inside this circle, energy is raised, rituals are performed, and spells are worked. This consecrated space is also where you call upon the gods and goddesses and become attuned to your own special deities. With attention and focus, working in the circle can be a wonderfully intense experience. All your senses will come alive. You will feel, see, and hear the energies you invoke. You will have created a tangible sphere of power.

You can, and doubtlessly will, cast a circle anywhere—out in the forest, on a beach, or in the comfort of your home. Wherever the circle is cast, that space becomes your temple. In your kitchen, stack the chairs against the wall to define the limits of your circle. Wiccan tradition specifies that the circle must have a diameter of nine feet (2.75m). We urban pagans might have less space, so you can extend into the closest room. I have had kitchens that more closely resembled large closets, so I would expand into the dining area and living room. The more rooms that are blessed, the better, I say! When you work outdoors with a large group of people, very large circles are cast. Many a witch casts a circle at the beginning of any spellwork and to enclose every sabbat celebration.

Casting a magical circle is only limited by your imagination or the purpose you ascribe to it. The magic begins at your will and with your hallowed tools. To be fully imbued with energy, your tools of magic and ritual should reside on your kitchen altar. Always cleanse and purify your newly acquired tools, whether they are antique or brand new. Think of your ritual tools as energy conductors that absorb and project the energy of the environment and the ritual work you perform. So, keep them clean, clear, and positive.

A Kitchen Witch's Toolkit

You'll find that you already own some of the kitchen witch's basic tools, but you may want to acquire new-to-you items whose sole use will be for kitchen magic.

BROOM ETIQUETTE

This is very important—do not use your ritual broom for housecleaning. Like me, you may well view every inch of your home as sacred space, but you will need to keep your regular housekeeping implements separate from those you use for your magical workings. Think of it as a separation of church and state, if you will. It pretty much is!

In general, it is not advisable to use tools such as your ritual knife to debone a chicken, for example, as this risks a confusing blending of mundane and magical energies. If you treat your ritual tools with the utmost respect, they will serve you very well. Over time, they will become inculcated with magic through exclusive use in your ritual workings. The Wiccan tradition holds brooms in high regard, and some witches have an impressive collection of brooms, each one named to distinguish their roles as "familiars," or kindred spirits. Kitchen witches often have the most extensive bevy of brooms of anyone.

Broom

This magical tool was born centuries ago from the practical magic of sweeping the ritual area clean before casting a spell. With focus and intention, you can dispel negative influences and bad spirits from the area and prepare a space for ritual work. In bygone days, pagan marriages and Beltane trysts took place with a leap over the broom, an old-fashioned tradition of handfasting, the classic witch wedding. Over the centuries, this rich history began to capture the imagination as the archetypal symbol of witches.

Your broom is an essential tool for energy management. Obtain a handmade broom from a craft fair or your favorite metaphysical five-and-dime. This should not be a machine-made plastic one from the supermarket, although I did get a long cinnamon-infused rush broom from Trader Joe's that I use in my witch's kitchen. A broom made of wood and woven of natural straw will be imbued with the inherent energies of those organic materials.

Crafting Your Own Purification Broom

To purify your space with as much of your own personal energy as possible, a broom you have crafted by hand is best. You don't have to wait until you are holding a circle or performing spellcraft—you can purify after a squabble with a loved one, to rid yourself of a bout of the blues, or any upset you need to sweep right out of your home. Many a kitchen witch begins the day with this simple ritual of a clean sweep to freshen surroundings and to make room for good energy in your life. Of course, this cleaning is not intended to make your house spotless; it is a symbolic act that is effective in maintaining your home as a personal sanctuary.

You can make your own purification broom from straw bound together and attached to a fallen tree branch, or you can add some mojo to a store-bought broom. Wrap copper wire around the bottom of your broom handle and also use it to bind straw to a sturdy stick or branch for the DIY kind. Venus-ruled copper lends an aura of beauty and keeps negativity at bay. Attach crystals to the handle with glue to boost your broom's power. Recommended crystals for space clearing and purification are as follows:

* **Amber** for good cheer

* **Blue lace agate** for tranquility and a peaceful home

* **Coral** for wellbeing

* **Jet** absorbs bad energy

* **Onyx** is a stone of protection

* **Petrified wood** for security

* **Tiger's eye** will protect you from energy-draining situations or people

* **Turquoise** creates calm and relaxation

Cauldron

Here we have a true essential for kitchen witchery! The cauldron represents the goddess; its round basin is symbolic of the womb from which we all came. Ideally made of cast iron or another durable metal that heats uniformly, the cauldron can hold fire and represents rebirth, the phoenix rising from the ashes of the past. Usually, cauldrons stand on three legs for practicality, stability, and mobility. You can place one on your kitchen altar if there is room or on the floor to the left of the altar.

In spring, this sacred basin can be used to hold earth or water and, in the winter season, it should hold fire—candle flames or sweet-smoked incense, which signifies the rebirth of the sun to come at the end of the coldest season. You can also be playful with the form the cauldron takes and use a rain-filled urn or a flower-filled fountain. Summer's cauldron can be a beautiful cup; at harvest-time, use a pumpkin or another hollowed-out gourd. You can play with the vessel concept in your own ceremonies and be imaginative—get really creative.

A classic cast-iron cauldron is very useful for mixing your herbs and essential oils—just make sure to clean it thoroughly after each use so as not to mix energies inadvertently. You can scry with a cauldron full of water to foresee the future by reading images on the surface of the water, as well as use this magical vessel for burning papers upon which you have written spells, incantations, and magical intentions. In doing this, you are sending your wishes to the gods and goddesses through the flames, the element of Fire.

Chalice

The chalice—another vessel symbolizing the feminine, the Goddess and fertility—is a goblet dedicated specially for use on your altar. Holding both physical fluid and waters of our emotional body, it is connected to the element of Water. Place your carefully chosen chalice on the left side of your altar with all other representations of the energy of the female and the Goddess. A grail is also a chalice. Legend tells that the Holy Grail brought life back to the decaying kingdom of Camelot and restored King Arthur and his people to health, giving rise to the rebirth of England itself. On your altar, your chalice can hold water, mead, wine, juice, or anything that has been blessed. It can contain holy water for consecrations and blessing rites. At the end of many ritual ceremonies and sabbats, it is customary to toast the deities with a hearty ale, cider, or wine and thank them for being present. After the circle has been opened, you can pour the contents of your chalice into the ground outdoors as an offering to benevolent entities.

Magic Bottles

Spell bottles, or magic bottles, have been around since the 1600s and were often filled with hair, nails, blood, and other kind of ephemera. Now, they are used to empower us and adorn our sacred spaces. Though their popularity has waned since the Elizabethan age when they were called "witch bottles," they are still used for a variety of intentions, and your magical kitchen can display many a spell bottle. You can customize your own spell-in-a-bottle with crystal stoppers and you should let your imagination run wild as to the usage and positive purposes with which you can fill your vessels: put one in your garden to keep your plants healthy, one in the bedroom to bring love and happiness, and a spell bottle on the living room mantel to protect your home. Spell bottles are used for protection primarily, but you can also put symbols of your dreams and desires in them—cinnamon for the spice of life, a rose for romance, rosemary for remembrance.

SPELL BOTTLE SECRETS

To ensure that your kitchen is peaceful, secure, and grounded in "good vibrations," gather a teaspoon of clean, dry soil from outside your home and put it into a bottle with smoky quartz crystal, brown jasper, or any dark, earthen-colored semiprecious stone. Place the bottle in a potted herb on your windowsill and think about the sanctity of your space every time you water your plant. As your plant grows and thrives, so will the tranquility of your space.

A bottle with a rosebud or rose petal, rose essential oil, and rose quartz next to your bedside will help with love. For six days, rub oil from the bottle onto a pink candle and burn it for one hour. On the seventh day, your romantic prospect will brighten.

For luck with money, place three pennies and some pyrite, green jade, or peridot in a bottle and put it on your desk or workspace. At least three times a day, visualize a lot of money and shake the magic money bottle. After three days, your fortunes will improve.

Bowls

While a bowl is not a tool in and of itself, you can utilize bowls in your spell work often and anytime you are inspired to do so. Clear, glass bowls are regularly used.

Blessing Bowl Ritual

These waters cleanse my
soul and being,
Now, with a clear mind and
heart, I am seeing,
I am love; my heart is as big
as sky and earth.
From the east to the west,
love universal gives life its worth.
Blessings to all, so mote it be.

Three simple ingredients—a red rose, a pink candle, and water—can bestow a powerful blessing. The rose signifies beauty, potential, the sunny seasons, love for yourself and others. The candle stands for the element of Fire, the yellow flame of the rising sun in the east, harmony, higher intention, and the light of the soul. Water represents its own element, flow, the direction of the west, emotions, and cleansing. This ritual can be performed alone or with a group in which you pass the bowl around.

Float the rose in a clear bowl of water and light a pink candle beside the bowl. With your left hand, gently stir the water in the bowl and say the words on the left.

Athame

Pronounced "a-tha-may," this is your magical knife. It can also be a ritual dagger or sword. The athame represents and contains yang energy, the male aspect of the deities. Ritual knifes are also associated with the element of Fire. For these two reasons, your ritual knife should be placed on the right side of your altar. It is to be used to direct the energies raised in your circles and spellwork; because it is not used for cutting but rather for the manipulation of the forces involved in the work of enchantment, an athame is usually a dull blade. The knives you use to slice bread and chop veggies are in a completely different category. Some Wiccan traditionalists specify that the handle of the athame should be black or very dark in color (as in the artwork to the right), since black is the color that absorbs energies and, therefore, becomes quickly attuned to the practitioner.

Bolline

A bolline, pronounced "bowl-in," is most often a white-handled knife (as in the artwork above right) that is used for making other tools and for cutting materials such as cords and herbs within the sacred circle. You can create your own magic wand, for example, by cutting a tree branch with your bolline. This increases the energy held within the wand and creates a magical tool by using a magical tool. You can also use your bolline for carving symbols and names into your candles and wands as well as your other tools. A bolline generally has a curved blade and a white handle to distinguish it from the athame, and it is also associated with male energy.

Wand

A magical wand is a powerful tool used to cast the circle and invoke deities. Like an athame, a wand focuses projects and directs energy. Because it gathers and stores magical power, a wand is wonderful for healing and can be the device with which you draw the shape when you cast the circle.

If possible, find your wand in a serendipitous manner. Draw it to yourself through attraction. A wand makes a mighty gift. If it feels really right to you, you can and should purchase your own wand. Just be sure to purify it, cleansing the energy of the shop so it is truly yours. However, before you take off for the next metaphysical five-and-dime, take a walk in the woods closest to where you reside. You may very well find the wand of your dreams waiting for you on the forest floor. Some folks prefer "live" wood such as cherry, willow, or oak branches that need to be cut off the tree. As a card-carrying eco-pagan, I vastly prefer fallen branches that nature has already harvested. Magical metals—copper, gold, and silver—are excellent for ornamenting your wand, and you may also want to adorn it with gems and crystals. The most important factor for any wand is how it "feels" in your hand. You will know immediately when you have found the right one.

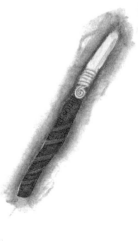

Candles

The popularity of candles has reached an all-time high. Candles are used by folks from all walks of life for relaxation, meditation, aromatherapy, and, most importantly, to achieve that "peaceful homey" feeling of being in your own sanctuary. This simple yet profound tool can make powerful magic. Take a moment and notice how candlelight transforms a dark room and fills the atmosphere with the energy of magical light. Suddenly the potential for transformation is evident. Every candle contains all four elements:

Air—Oxygen feeds and fans the candle flame
Earth—Solid wax forms the body of the candle
Water—Melting wax represents the fluid elemental state
Fire—The flame sparks and blazes

How to Charge a Candle

Charging a candle means instilling it with magical intent. A candle that has been charged fills your personal space with intention and expands it into all four elements and into the celestial sphere. Ritual candles are chosen for their color correspondences and are carved, "dressed," or anointed with special oils chosen for their particular energy.

Once you clarify your intention, cleanse your candles by passing them through the purifying smoke of sage or incense. Further charge your candle by carving a symbol into the wax. You can warm the tip of your ritual knife using a lit match and carve your full intention into the candle wax. As you engrave the appropriate magical works onto the candle, you are charging it with energy and the hope and purpose of your spell. Some highly successful examples of this that I have used and witnessed in circle gatherings are: "Healing for my friend who is in the hospital; she will recover with renewed and increased health." "I get the raise I am asking for, and more!" "New true love enters my life in the coming season, blessed be."

Next, you should "dress" your candle with a specific oil. Every essential oil is imbued with a power that comes from the plants and flowers of which it is made. You can also use oils to anoint yourself at the crown of the head

A QUICK GUIDE TO CANDLE-COLOR MAGIC

Green: money, prosperity, growth, luck, jobs, gardening, youth, beauty, fertility

Dark blue: change, flexibility, the unconscious, psychic powers, emotional healing

Pink: love, friendship, kindness, faithfulness, goodness, affection

Brown: home, animal wisdom, grounding, physical healing

Black: banishes, absorbs, expels the negative, heals serious illness

Gold: solar magic, money, attraction, the astral plane

Orange: the law of attraction, success with legal issues, mutability, stimulation, support, encouragement, joy

Light blue: patience, happiness, triumph over depression, calm, deep understanding, compassion

Red: strength, protection, sexuality, vitality, passion, courage, heart, intense feelings of love, good health, power

White: purification, peace, protection from negativity, truth, binding, sincerity, serenity, chastity, gladness, spirit

Purple: female power, stress relief, ambition, healing past wounds, goddess-hood, business success

Gray: neutrality, impasses, cancellation

Yellow: mental power and vision, intelligence, clear thinking, study, self-assurance, prosperity, divination, psychism, abundance, wisdom, power of persuasion, charisma, sound sleep

or at the third eye to increase mental clarity. By using the inherent powers of essential oils and anointing both your tool and yourself, you are increasing and doubling the energies, in this case the candle and yourself.

Essential oils are highly concentrated extracts of flowers, herbs, roots, or resin extract, sometimes diluted in neutral-base oil. Try to ensure you are using natural oils instead of manufactured, chemical-filled perfume oil; the synthetics lack any real energy. Also, approach oils with caution and don't get them in your eyes. Clean cotton gloves are a good idea to keep in your witch's kitchen for handling sensitive materials. You can avoid any mess and protect your magical tools by using oil droppers. Do not use essential oils in the first trimester of pregnancy and consult an aromatherapist if using in the later stages. Find a trusted herbalist or the wise sage at your local metaphysical shop; usually they can offer much in the way of helpful knowledge. I have included as much as I can in the following at-a-glance guide to oils.

Magical Meanings of Essential Oils

* **Healing:** bay, cedar wood, cilantro (coriander), cinnamon, eucalyptus, juniper, lime, rose, sandalwood, spearmint

* **Prosperity:** aloe, basil, cinnamon, clove, ginger, nutmeg, oakmoss, orange, patchouli, peppermint, pine

* **Love:** apricot, basil, chamomile, cilantro (coriander), clove, copal, geranium, jasmine, lemon, lime, neroli, rose, rosemary, ylang-ylang

* **Sexuality:** amber, cardamom, clove, lemongrass, olive, patchouli, rose

* **Peace:** chamomile, lavender

* **Luck:** nutmeg, orange, rose, vervain

* **Courage:** black pepper, frankincense, geranium

* **Joy:** bergamot, lavender, neroli, vanilla

* **Divination:** camphor, clove, orange

* **Astral projection:** benzoin, cinnamon, jasmine, sandalwood

* **Dispelling negative energy and spirits:** basil, clove, copal, frankincense, juniper, myrrh, peppermint, pine, rosemary, Solomon's seal, vervain, yarrow

* **Protection:** anise, bay, black pepper, cedar wood, clove, copal, cypress, eucalyptus, frankincense, juniper, lavender, lime, myrrh, rose geranium, sandalwood, vetiver

* **Enchantment:** amber, apple, ginger, tangerine

Censer

A censer, pronounced "sen-ser" and also known as a thurible, is an incense burner and represents the elements of Air and Fire. Place your incense at the very center of your altar. Incense is way to bless your space and also to purify with the sacred smoke—your tools, your ritual circle, your mind. The evocative scent and soft, billowing smoke will transport you in a sensory way. Nowadays, there is an incredible variety of incense burners available, so follow your instincts as to what is best for your kitchen altar—perhaps a smoking dragon or a goddess holding the fiery embers of your incense would add greatly to the energy of your altar.

It is a good idea to test your incense before using it in ritual, especially before organizing a group circle, to see how much smoke is produced to avoid any problems; and it's best to check with your fellow participants to make sure no one has any special sensitivities. One of my dearest and nearest gets migraines whenever any amber is used—candles, oils, incense. If you find you can't burn incense for any such reason, you can use another Air symbol instead, such as feathers, potpourri, fresh flowers, or even a paper fan.

Incense itself contains inherent energies that you can use to

TWENTY-FIRST CENTURY PAGAN POWER TOOLS

For really big batches of incense, try using a blender or food processor. This "modern pagan" approach will save a lot of time and elbow grease. This can really come in handy when you are preparing for high-holiday celebrations with large groups or making gifts for witchy friends.

augment your intention and further power your magical purpose. I have learned much about different kinds of incense—loose, cone, stock, and cylinder, as well as the best kinds of herbs to use from experimentation, asking elders, and observing magi at work. Following are two of my favorite incense recipes.

Circle Incense

4 *parts frankincense*

2 *parts myrrh*

2 *parts benzoin*

1 *part sandalwood*

1 *part cinnamon*

1 *part rose petals*

1 *part vervain*

1 *part rosemary*

1 *part bay leaf*

1 *part orange peel*

This incense will significantly aid the formation of the sphere of energy that is the ritual circle (see page 25). Each part is a heaping teaspoon in my recipes but you can change that if you are making larger batches. A fine grind of all the ingredients is the key to good incense, so you should add a pestle and mortar to your kitchen if you plan to make a lot of incense.

Clearing Incense

3 *parts myrrh*

3 *parts copal*

3 *parts frankincense*

1 *part sandalwood*

This is an optimal mixture of essences to purify your home or sacred working space. Negative energies are vanquished and the path is cleared for ritual. Open windows and doors when you are burning this cleaning incense so the bad can be released outside and dissipate. It is advisable to use this recipe if there are arguments or any other kind of disruptions in your home. You can create sanctuary with this incense.

Book of Shadows

Here we have your kitchen witch's recipe record, a ledger for all your magical workings, including spells, rituals, and results. This is your journal of all you have practiced and wrought as well as your research. Are your spells more effective during the new moon in the water signs of Cancer, Pisces, or Scorpio? That may well be unique to you and as you arrive at these important discoveries, you should write them down in your Book of Shadows so you know your true power as tested by time. This is not just a ledger though, it is a living document that you can apply to magical workings to come and will even help you design your own spells and ritual recipes. All the astrology, herb lore, crystal properties, lunar signs, and seasonal information will come into play as you experiment and uncover what works best for you. By keeping my own Book of Shadows, I was able to conclude that, for me, the new moon in Pisces is a super-powered time for my spells.

This is a book you will turn to again and again and your Book of Shadows should be very appealing to you. It can be a gorgeous, one-of-a-kind volume made with handmade paper and uniquely tooled bindings, or it can be a simple three-ring binder. Whatever is most useful to you.

Coming Full Circle

"The human heart longs for ritual—to be fully alive and whole. We must engage in rites of passage."

Chapter 3

Succulent Spells
for Magical Meals

Preparing and sharing food can be ceremonial, be it on a
Tuesday school night or during the festivals of the season.
With kitchen witchery, a simple bowl of savory soup can
be the equal of a Samhain feast; the ingredients, the
astrological aspects, phases of the moon, words spoken,
and your intention make it so. Cooking is a magical act
and serving your family and friends is to serve the gods.
Learning about and utilizing the properties of certain
herbs, spices, and ingredients as you practice this sacred
culinary art is an enormous source of happiness you will
pass on to all at your table.

Magical Cookery

The kitchen is the heart center of every home. No matter how beautifully we decorate parlors, living rooms, and dens, people gravitate right back to the kitchen. Why is that? Kitchens are where the magic happens! Food is made here and, along with it, plenty of love is dished up in heaping servings. With kitchen witchery, recipes and preparations go into spellwork, concocting cures right out of the cupboard, preserving and canning food grown in the garden, drying herbs for teas and cookery, and unleashing the power of the pantry. In creating enchanted edibles, we can use the best and freshest ingredients for healthy, hearty dishes, but we can also add in some very special ingredients with our magical intention in accordance with the celestial calendar and by utilizing the ingredients with the desired properties. In the words of the great Wiccan teacher Scott Cunningham, "Since lemons have been used for centuries in purifying rituals, can't we bake a lemon pie and internalize its cleansing energies?"

I had the great good fortune to grow up in the countryside on a farm. Much of what I know I learned from my witchy aunt—about which herbs to gather in the wild, which foods to cook for love, money, luck, health, and in celebration of the high holidays. It is exciting to go to the garden, the grocery store, or the farmer's market and bring home the ingredients for positive life change. In addition to the secrets to magical cooking, I learned from this wise woman that the first task to undertake is to clean your kitchen and purify it. If anything needs repairing, fix it. Any utensils, pots, or pans that are dented can be donated. If your kitchen curtains look shabby to your eye, make or buy new ones. If there is a bag of rice or beans past its prime, compost away. You should clean the cooking space in both the practical sense and also cleanse it in the magical sense. Prepare your kitchen to be used for the purpose of magic.

Harvest Moon Herb Soup

After the September equinox signals the change of seasons from summer to fall, you should start making pots of this seasonal meal, which is a guaranteed crowd pleaser. This autumnal soup is just as pleasing to the cook as it can be a quick supper, leftovers for lunch, and easily frozen for meals on the go. It is simple and delicious. On the eve of the first full moon of fall, gather the ingredients and prepare. Refrigerate overnight and the flavors will "marry" together to intensify and become an even more savory supper to serve to loved ones on this harvest moon night.

In a large iron skillet or frying pan (preferably well-seasoned by use in your kitchen) fry the leeks in the olive oil until they become soft and translucent. Add in the chopped garlic and cook until it is also soft and wafting a wonderful scent into your kitchen. Transfer to a soup pot, oil and all,

3 large leeks, thinly sliced

¼ cup (60ml) virgin olive oil

2 fresh garlic cloves, chopped

8 cups (2 liters) water

1 butternut squash, peeled, seeded, and coarsely grated

1 carrot, thinly sliced

4 large floury potatoes, such as Idaho or Maris Piper, or sweet potatoes, peeled and cut into small, spoon-sized chunks

¼ cup (5g) fresh sage, finely chopped

¼ cup (10g) fresh chives, finely chopped

Salt and pepper

¼ teaspoon celery salt

Serves 8

and add the water, heating to a boil. Add all the veggies and herbs and turn the heat down to a simmer for 45 minutes. Test the potatoes to see if they are soft enough—do this by mashing with a wooden spoon. If they are still a bit hard, simmer for another 5 minutes. Turn the heat down very low, then season with salt and pepper. Add the celery salt as the last element of the year's abundance.

Serve in clay, wooden, or ceramic bowls by the light of a brown or yellow candle. A chunk of homemade bread would be the ideal seasonal accompaniment.

Moon Drop Savory Scones

1 cup (125g) all-purpose (plain) flour

¼ teaspoon baking soda (bicarbonate of soda)

1 teaspoon baking powder

¼ teaspoon salt

3 tablespoons (40g) cold unsalted butter

⅔ cup (160ml) buttermilk

Makes 10 biscuits

Serve these piping hot and straight out of the oven; this is a batch of ten delicious biscuits (scones). Better still, they're drop biscuits, which means there's no need to roll and cut the dough. If you are having more than five folks over for supper, double up the ingredients. These Moon Drop biscuits are excellent for dipping into soup and stews.

Preheat the oven to 450°F/230°C/gas mark 8. In a medium bowl, combine the flour, baking soda, baking powder, and salt. Whisk gently to blend the ingredients. With two knives, cut the butter in until the mixture looks like coarse meal. Add in the buttermilk and stir until it is blended, but do not over stir. Drop heaping tablespoons of the mixture onto an oiled baking sheet; you should separate the biscuits by 2 inches (5cm). Bake for 12 minutes and pull the biscuits out once they are a light-golden, buttery brown.

LET THE NIGHT SKY BE YOUR GUIDE

The proper phase of the moon is essential for spellcraft in the art of kitchen witchery. The waning moon is the time to wind down any personal challenges and see them to an end. The new moon is an auspicious time for a fresh start. While waxing, the moon grows steadily larger and is good for spellwork's fruition. The full moon is a great teacher with a special message for each month.

Lunar Lore

Many of our full-moon names come from medieval books of hours and also from the Native American tradition. Here is a list of rare names from the two traditions, which you may want to use in your lunar rituals.

* **January:** Old Moon, Chaste Moon; this fierce Wolf Moon is the time to recognize your strength of spirit

* **February:** Hunger Moon; the cool Snow Moon is for personal vision and intention-setting

* **March:** Crust Moon, Sugar Moon; the gentle Sap Moon heralds the end of winter and nature's rebirth

* **April:** Sprouting Grass Moon, Egg Moon, Fish Moon; spring's sweet Pink Moon celebrates health and full life force

* **May:** Milk Moon, Corn Planting Moon, Dyad Moon; the Flower Moon provides inspiration with the bloom of beauty

* **June:** Hor Moon, Rose Moon; the Strawberry Moon heralds the Summer Solstice and sustaining power of the sun

* **July:** Buck Moon, Hay Moon; this Thunder Moon showers us with rain and cleansing storms

* **August:** Barley Moon, Wyrt Moon, Sturgeon Moon; summer gifts us with the Red Moon, the time for passion and lust for life

* **September:** Green Corn Moon, Wine Moon; fall's Harvest Moon is the time to be grateful and reap what we have sown

* **October:** Dying Grass Moon, Travel Moon, Blood Moon, Moon of Changing Seasons; the Hunter's Moon is when we plan and store for winter ahead

* **November:** Frost Moon, Snow Moon; Beaver Moon is the time to call upon our true wild nature

* **December:** Cold Moon, Oak Moon; this is the lightest night of the shortest day and is the time to gather the tribe around the fire and share stories of the good life together

May Magic: Flower Moon Invocation

The fullest phase of the moon can be the time for the greatest of magic—you can conjure your heart's desire and tackle the "big things" of life, whether that be a problem to resolve, a major life transition, such as seeking a new job or home, whatever your truest wish. This gorgeous spring Flower Moon provides an optimal opportunity to strive for the new, to initiate a phase of transformation in your life that will last long after the full moon has waxed into darkness. This invocation honors the season of spring, planting seeds of positive change in your life that will bloom for years to come. Start by gathering red and green apples, candles of the same colors, a few grains of seed corn from a gardening store or natural grocery, along with three stalks of lavender and a long strand night-blooming jasmine. Leave these offerings on your altar all day.

Through the power of Earth and Air,
Water and Fire.
As I bite this fruit of knowledge,
I am thus inspired.
All possibilities are before me. And so it is.

When the full moon of May reaches the highest point in the night sky, light one red and one green candle on your kitchen altar. Wind the jasmine and lavender into a crown for the top of your head, breathing in the lovely scent the flowers produce. For three minutes, visualize your desired change for this spell. Holding an apple in each hand, speak the words of the spell on the left while circling the candlelit altar clockwise three times.

Eat from both apples until you are fully satisfied, then bury the corn seeds and the cores near your kitchen door or the rightmost corner of your garden. With the spring rains, your intentions will come into being. By the fall full moon, you will be harvesting the bounty of change from this spell, with great gratitude.

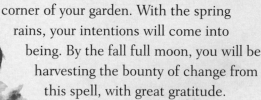

Basil Pesto Perfection

This recipe is simply scrumptious and a bargain to boot. You can gather a nice big bunch of basil leaves from your kitchen garden or greengrocer.

Rinse the leaves in cold water and place them on a clean dish towel to air dry. Place the pine nuts and the garlic on a baking sheet in the oven at 375°F/190°C/gas mark 5 for 5–10 minutes or until the pine nuts begin to turn slightly golden. Do not wait until they turn brown, though.

Place the pine nuts and garlic in a blender or food processor with the Parmesan. Before you put the lid in place, cut the lemon in half and squeeze out a nice dollop of fresh juice and grind in a healthy dash of sea salt. Blend away until you have a lovely green pesto sauce you can put on anything. Perfect pesto in 10 minutes flat!

Based on the benefits of this herb, it might be the perfect dish to serve up after an emotionally hard week, as it is a bringer of peace. Also good for date night or when you need to brew up some good money-mojo. Boil up a pot of pasta while you are concocting the blissful basil and you will have a sumptuous weeknight supper for the family on the table so quickly, they will be sure you are using witchcraft!

2 cups (100g) packed fresh basil leaves

½ cup (70g) pine nuts

3 garlic cloves, peeled

½ cup (50g) Parmesan cheese, grated

Juice of ½ fresh lemon

Sea salt

Serves 6

Basil Abundance Ritual

With bounteous hand and healthful balm,
Blessed basil, most verdurous herb,
Bring me health and heart and calm,
Abundance I shall see by every
deed and verb.
And so it is.

Take a few sprigs of basil before you cook and put them in a green bowl on your kitchen altar. Boil water as for tea and pour over the herb in the bowl. Now chant the medieval-inspired charm on the left.

Breathe in the steam from the basil bowl and fill your lungs with the smell of prosperity. Repeat the spell once more, then leave the basil bowl on your altar for 24 hours. Not only will your thinking be greatly clarified but you will also begin to see signs of your wealth increasing within one week. With basil flourishing in your herb pots, you have a ready source bursting with positive money energy.

Savory Sweet Potato Mooncakes

2 large semi-baked sweet
potatoes, peeled and grated

1 large carrot, grated

3 eggs

½ tablespoon dried rosemary

½ tablespoon dried sage

½ cup (120ml) olive oil

1 cup (240ml) organic
natural yogurt

Fresh chives

Makes 8 mooncakes

Hearty and oh-so-healthy, these pancakes make for a marvelous full-moon meal. Sweet potatoes are truly beneficial to women's health and contain estrogen; these tubers are good for you inside and outside as they also give your skin a nice boost. But their main magic for everyone is that they are a vehicle for grounding. Anytime you feel spacey or out-of-sorts or distracted, this food will serve you well.

Mix the potatoes and carrot in a large bowl. Beat the eggs and add to the veggie mixture and mix thoroughly. Grind the rosemary and sage to a very fine powder in your mortar and pestle. Add the herbs to the veggie mixture, plus salt and pepper to taste. Shape into round balls, enough for eight mooncakes. Warm the oil slowly in a skillet/frying pan until it is hot. Place the balls in the oil and flatten into rounds with a spatula. Cook through for 8 minutes on each side or until they are golden brown and beginning to crisp on both sides. Plate up and top with organic yogurt and chives. If you are feeling decadent, dollop on sour cream and enjoy with a circle of friends under the sheen of a bright and holy moon.

Parsley Potato Salad

Parsley has somehow become just a garnish, but it is actually the perfect party herbage as it is ruled by both Mercury and Venus and brings eloquence and extra charm. As a bonus, it helps to reduce drunkenness and is a proven breath freshener. Potatoes are centering and connote the prosperity principle of stability. Waxy potatoes, such as new potatoes, are optimal, especially those grown by your own hand, but floury potatoes are fine here, too. Potato salad should not wait for picnics and parties, it is marvelous for any meal and quite economical, too.

Boil the cubed potatoes in a pan of water for 20 minutes, then drain. While the potatoes are cooling, place them in a large bowl and add in the onion. Whisk the lemon, vinegar, mustard, and sugar together and pour in the olive oil, bit by bit. Pour most of the herbs and dressing into the still-warm potatoes and stir until the dressing is completely mixed in. Season to taste and top with the remaining herbs. This dish is a lovely-tasting reminder of how the earth sustains us all.

6 large scrubbed-clean potatoes, cubed (skin on for more nutrients)

1 large red onion, finely chopped

Juice of 1 lemon

2 tablespoons apple cider vinegar

4 tablespoons mustard

1 tablespoon granulated sugar

¾ cup (180ml) olive oil

½ cup (20g) each fresh parsley and chives (a nice bunch from the garden)

Serves 6

Peace and Love Nut Roastie

1 white onion, chopped

½ stick (55g) unsalted butter

2 cups (280g) mixed nuts

8 ounces (225g) day-old bread

1½ cups (350ml) vegetable stock

1 teaspoon dried sage

Salt and pepper

Soy or tamari sauce

Serves 10

Nuts are one of the healthiest things we humans can eat, packed with positive proteins, beneficial oils, and very tasty. This nearly effortless nut roastie is a great snack for movie night at home, party time, and makes a savory appetizer for special meals.

Preheat the oven to 350°F/180°C/gas mark 4. Sauté the onion in the butter until it softens. Mix the nuts together with the bread in a food processor until blended well, then transfer to a large bowl. Heat the stock to boiling point and pour into the mixture in the bowl. Stir in the onion. Season as you see fit with sage, salt, and pepper. Pour in a tablespoon of the soy or tamari sauce to add zing to your roast and give one last stir.

Spoon the roastie mix into a 15 x 10 x 2-inch (38 x 25 x 5-cm) greased baking dish and bake for 30 minutes. Notice as your kitchen fills with a fantastic aroma. Heating the nuts brings out more of their natural oils and intensifies the flavor. Like herbs and flowers, nuts have magical properties that help increase love and also feelings of conviviality and peace, thus the name of this dish. When you serve this roastie, you are quite literally "sharing the love."

Rite of Connection

Before you enjoy this friendly repast together, hold hands and recite:

Sister, brother, tribe of the soul, ones who care.
Merry may we meet again to share.
Breaking bread and quaffing mead
We draw closer in word and deed.
Blessing of love to all!

Nurturing Nettle Soup

Nettles are a hedge witch favorite for all their qualities as a healing plant, bringing good cheer, and for their usefulness in breaking hexes. They are also a green that can be used as you might use kale or watercress. They were regarded and used as a superfood by wise women for centuries and are packed with Vitamin A, iron, and have a high protein count. They are best harvested when they are young in the springtime. Nevertheless, they are an excellent element in cookery year around and have a surprisingly delicate flavor. They are another generous genus as they sprout up and reseed themselves as true gifts from Mother Earth. Try this old-time recipe and you will soon be out hunting nettles in the wild so you can enjoy this medieval meal at all times. Beware: nettles are called "stinging" for good reason, so wear rubber gloves when you are working with them to be on the safe side.

Start cooking the pre-soaked peas in a large pan with just enough water to cover. Once they have boiled, keep them on a high simmer. Keep an eye on them while you cook the onions and garlic to transparency in the olive oil in a skillet/frying pan. Add water to the peas as needed and cook for 35 minutes or until they have softened; now add the veggie stock or yeasty water.

Add the softened garlic and onions to the bean pot and simmer on low for 25 minutes. Add the nettles to the big pot and cook for a further 30 minutes. Season to taste and share this nurturing soup. Make sure to give thanks to the guardian spirits of the earth for this gift of great greens.

1 cup (165g) black-eyed peas (black-eyed beans), washed and soaked in water overnight

3 yellow onions, chopped

2 garlic cloves, chopped

¼ cup (60ml) olive oil

3 cups (720ml) vegetable stock

2 cups (200g) nettles, washed thoroughly with tougher stalks discarded, chopped

celery salt, salt, and pepper

Serves 8

*

PENNY STOCKS

Buying premade stock at the grocer can be very expensive. You can save a lot of money by dissolving a tablespoon of yeast in 3 cups (720ml) warm water to arrive at a delicious starter for soups and stews. This recipe costs almost nothing.

Goddess Greens

2 cups (150g) fresh kale or chard (with a suggested side of nettle)

2 small garlic cloves

2 tablespoons olive oil

2 tablespoons red pepper flakes, plus ½ teaspoon to garnish

1 tablespoon apple cider vinegar

Garlic salt

Serves 6

This dish should be the gardener's choice with a big bunch of gorgeous greens.

Wash the greens thoroughly, chop, and set aside. Peel and mash the garlic cloves. Heat the olive oil in a skillet/frying pan and fry up the garlic and the pepper flakes. Add in the chopped greens and stir well. Cover the pan and lower the heat, giving a stir every few minutes. When the greens have softened to your liking, add in a tablespoon of the apple cider vinegar and a big dash of the garlic salt. Stir vigorously three times counterclockwise and pray to the great kitchen goddess who provides us with everything we have. Remove from the heat. Lift the lid and add half a teaspoon of red pepper flakes.

Serve this goddess-blessed dish of greens to people who claim not to like veggies or greens and you will delight and surprise quite a few. Be prepared to be asked for the recipe repeatedly. Every time you share the dish (or the recipe), you'll be sharing the gifts of the goddess directly.

Invoke Your Kitchen Goddess

The great Roman earth goddess Ceres is an excellent guardian of the garden and pantry; every time you pour a bowl of cereal for your loved one, you invoke her. Cerealia is an early summer festival held in southern Europe in her honor, celebrating the profusion of crops she will bring in from the fields. Any ceremony for planting, growing, and cooking can involve this bounty-bringer. If you are going to plant a magical garden, craft a ritual with Ceres, and make an altar to this grain goddess and, my, how your garden will grow! When you harvest and cook something you have grown, show your gratitude to her in prayer.

Ramped-Up Rice

As winter thaws into spring, bulbs are the first to do the work of bringing forth the new season. An old-fashioned food that is now wildly popular is ramps (wild garlic), formerly the domain of hill folk and farm-women. Even the chicest of city chefs have gone wild for ramps, which are akin to leeks and can substitute for each other in recipes. Ramps are more powerfully pungent. The beauty of this recipe is that rice and ramps take 20 minutes to cook. This change-of-seasons dish combines risotto-style rice with a harbinger of spring to delightful result. The old wives and hearth witches who were the first to explore ramps believed this healing green could prevent colds and flu.

In a heavy saucepan, melt the butter over moderate heat. Toss in the sliced ramp bulbs and cook for 3–5 minutes until they soften, stirring gently. Add the rice to the pan and stir well to mix the rice, butter, and ramps and get the rice sticky with butter. After 2 minutes, add the chicken stock, salt, and cayenne pepper and stir thoroughly. Bring to a boil, stir three times counterclockwise, and then turn the heat down low and let simmer for 20 minutes. At that point, all of the liquid should have been absorbed by the rice. Turn the heat off and add half of the minced ramp greens into the rice. Pour the ramped-up rice into a serving bowl and sprinkle the rest of the minced greens on the top as a garnish.

Before you and your guests begin, stop and breathe in the healing savory greens. This is also an occasion to share stories of the wise women and elders in your life and honor all they have passed down.

3 tablespoons unsalted butter

½ cup (75g) sliced ramp (wild garlic) bulbs

1½ cups (280g) long grain rice

3 cups (720ml) unsalted organic chicken stock

Salt

1 teaspoon cayenne pepper

½ cup (120ml) finely minced ramp (wild garlic) greens

Serves 6

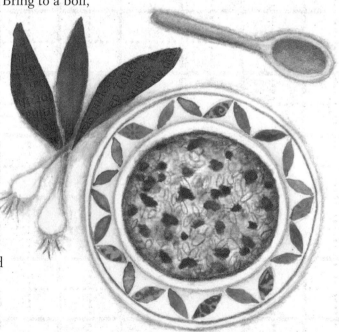

Witch's Cottage Pie

4–5 potatoes, boiled

1 tablespoon unsalted butter

Milk

Salt and pepper

2 tablespoons olive oil

1 yellow onion, chopped

2 cups (450g) ground
(minced) beef, or soy protein
for meat-free options

1 cup (120g) carrots, sliced

1 cup (75g) button
mushrooms, sliced

1 cup (150g) cherry tomatoes
(or 1¾ cups (400g) strained
tomatoes)

Herbs, such as parsley, sage, or
rosemary, chopped

½ cup (45g) Cheddar
cheese, grated

Serves 8

This recipe is pagan comfort food at its finest and is very filling and festive. Many of us kitchen witches are working mothers with very busy schedules, so this family favorite is good to double up on. Make one to serve piping hot out of the oven and freeze the second for an after-school and post-work reheated repast.

Preheat the oven to 375°F/190°C/gas mark 5. Mash the potatoes with the butter, adding a splash of milk until you have the desired consistency. Add salt and pepper to taste and make sure you can get peaks so the pie is impressively landscaped!

Slowly heat the olive oil in a sauté pan and cook the onions until soft, then fold in and cook the meat or veggie protein. Lastly, add in the carrots, mushrooms, and tomatoes and cook through. Season with salt and pepper to taste and add in your favorite herbs—parsley, sage, rosemary—whatever your heart desires.

Transfer to an oiled 3-quart/13 x 9 x 2-inch (2.7 liter/33 x 23 x 5-cm) casserole and spread evenly. Sprinkle the grated cheese on top. Lastly, spread the mashed potatoes on top, creating peaks and valleys. Dust a sprinkling of parsley and chives on top and pop into the oven for 15 minutes. Once the potato-mash topping begins to turn a lovely golden brown on top, remove from the oven. Serve this hearty homemade savory pie in bowls alongside a crisp salad of homegrown greens and allow the coziness to melt all the mundane matters away. Good for any day of the week and also impressive enough to bake for high holidays.

Magic Mushroom Quiche

5 eggs

½ cup (120ml) milk

Salt and pepper

1 cup (85g) cheese, grated; cook's choice of Cheddar, Swiss, or another family favorite

½ cup (75g) crimini or buttom mushrooms, sliced

Premade pastry lining a greased 9½-inch (24-cm) pie pan or quiche shell (can be store-bought or handmade, depending on how much time you have)

Sprigs of fresh rosemary

Serves 6

HARVEST YOUR HEALTH

Just what is so magical about mushrooms? Crimini mushrooms provide an excellent source of 15 different vitamins, minerals, and antioxidant phytonutrients. They have even been reported to be an anti-cancer food and aid in the reduction of high cholesterol. Mighty magical indeed!

This dish can be a main course served with a leafy green salad or a yummy hot breakfast or brunch with a side of fruit. Make two and your weekend options are deliciously open. You can also add greens such as nettles, spinach, or chives to add more color and nutrients to your meal.

Preheat your oven to 375°F/190°C/gas mark 5. Whisk the eggs and milk together and season with salt and pepper. Fold in the grated cheese and stir in the mushrooms. Pour the mixture into the pastry shell and pop into the oven for 35 minutes. When the top is turning a nice golden brown, remove the quiche from the oven and let it cool. Top with sprigs of aromatic fresh rosemary from your witch's garden.

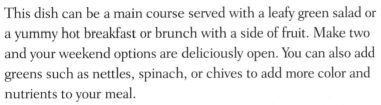

Coming Full Circle

"A kitchen witch preparing a ritual meal for her circle is engaging in one of the oldest forms of enchantment by harnessing the energies in each ingredient and cooking with sacred intention."

Chapter 4

Brewing up Blessings

Witch's brews are one of the most important aspects of
house magic. These tonics comprise many kinds of teas,
wines, ciders, and refreshments as well as medicinal
tinctures, tisanes, infusions, and herbal vinegars. Your
garden grows plants, herbs, and fruits that are the source
of delectable draughts and healing concoctions, which are
at the very heart of kitchen witchery. A pantry filled with
bottles of brew made by your own hand will be a constant
source of delight to you and your circle.

A Mug of Magic

The British and kitchen witches have one thing in common—they believe a good pot of tea can fix almost anything. And it is true—heartache, headaches, and all manner of ills seem to evaporate in the steam that rises from the spout of the kettle. With a handful of herbs and a cauldron-full of witchy wisdom, big healing can result from a small cup of tea. Once you have the knack of that, you can also brew up simples, digestives, tisanes, tonics, tinctures, and the many other concoctions that can be created right at home. This is one of the most delightful aspects of kitchen witchery as these recipes are usually easy enough as long as you have the proper ingredients. They make all the difference after a long day at the office; they can be enjoyed alone and can also be shared to great effect. Bottled and hand labeled, these potions also make significant gifts that will be long remembered for the thoughtfulness as well as the delight and comfort received. Prepare to brew up much joy.

Simples

Teas brewed from a single herb are commonly called simples, a lovely phrase from olden times. Experience has taught me that simples often have the most potency; the purity of that single plant essence can come through undiluted. This book contains a plentitude of herbs you can use to brew tasty, helpful, and healing simples, but yarrow is one you should brew regularly. Boil 2½ cups (590ml) of spring water. Place a half-ounce (15ml) of dried yarrow into your favorite crockery pot and pour over the water. Steep for 10 minutes and strain with a non-metallic implement, such as an inexpensive bamboo strainer or cheesecloth. Sweeten with honey; clover honey intensifies the positivity of this potion and makes it a supremely lucky drink. Yarrow brings courage, heart, and is a major medicine. All these aspects make yarrow one of the most strengthening of all simples.

Jasmine Joy Ritual

Jasmine tea is a delightful concoction and can create an aura of bliss and conviviality. It is available at any grocer or purveyor of organic goods, but homegrown is even better. Brew a cup of jasmine tea and let it cool. Add two parts lemonade to one part jasmine tea and drink the mixture with a good friend. Jasmine is a vine and represents the intertwining of people. You will be more bonded to anyone with whom you share this sweet ritual.

This is also a tonic that you can indulge in when alone. I recommend brewing up a batch every Monday, or "Moon Day," to ensure that each week is filled with joyfulness.

As the jasmine tea steeps, pray:

On this Moon Day in this new week,
I call upon the spirits to guide joy to my door.
By this moon on this day, I call upon Selene, goddess fair
To show me the best way to live.
For this, I am grateful.
Blessed be the brew; blessed be me.

✳ TELEPATHY TEA

The humble dandelion, abhorred by lawn keepers everywhere, hides its might very well. Dandelion root tea can call upon the spirit of anyone whose advice you might need. Simply place a freshly brewed simple using this herbal root on your bedroom altar or nightstand. Before you sleep, say the name of your helper aloud seven times. In a dream or vision, the spirit will visit you and answer all your questions. During medieval times, this spell was used to find hidden treasure. Chaucer, who was well-versed in astrology and other metaphysics, advised this tried and true tea.

Steeped in Wisdom

Different kinds of tea can combine to make a powerful concoction. A pot of your favorite grocer's black tea can become a magical potion with the addition of a thin slice of ginger root and a pinch each of dried chamomile and peppermint tea. This ambrosial brew can calm any storm at home or at work. Before you drink a cup, pray:

This day I pray for calm and serenity for all,
Both within and without.
Give me the wisdom to see the beauty of each waking moment.
Blessings abound to all I know.
So mote it be.

Gardener's Tea

2 parts dried echinacea

2 parts dried chamomile

1 part dried mint

1 part anise seed

1 part dried thyme

As you now know, tilling the back forty and harvesting your herbs, veggies, and weeding is a huge amount of work. It is one of life's greatest joys, without doubt, but nevertheless, many a sore back and aching knees have come as result of a thriving garden. All the more reason for tea that revives, refreshes, and offers relief to aching joints.

Gather the ingredients from your store of dried herbs, and add boiling water. Allow to steep, then strain into a cup. A nice hot cup of this remedy will have you jumping back into the garden to plant more of all the herbs that comprise this delightful tea. Ahh, sit back and enjoy. You deserve it!

Midsummer's Day Dream Tea Cooler

Not every herbal tea will work over ice, but this one will have your family and friends clamoring for more. Gather a handful of these dried herbs:

1 part each of lemon verbena, lemon balm, mint, chamomile, and hibiscus

2 cups (480ml) peach juice

1 lemon

Place the herbs in a pot, pour over 6 cups (1.5 liters) of boiling water, and let cool to room temperature. Pour into a large pitcher and add the peach juice to two thirds full. Give a good stir and add in enough ice cubes to fill the container. Slice the lemon and lay on top. Serve, sit back, and let the compliments begin. This convivial concoction is ideal for special summer occasions, such as the midsummer celebration of the solstice.

Prayer to Honor the Summer

For summer festivals, such as the Summer Solstice on June 21 (see page 128), you should honor the deities who gift us with such plenty. Light yellow and green candles at your altar and on the feast table and offer this appeal:

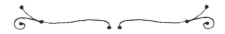

Oh, Lady of Summer
Who brings sun and life-giving rains,
May each harvest bring the crops that fill our cups.
The rivers and oceans, fields and farms are yours.
We honor you today and give thanks to you for all we have.
A toast to thee, blessed be!

Dandelion Divination Wine

14 ounces (400g) freshly picked and cleaned dandelion blossoms (no stems or leaves)

1 orange and 1 lemon, thinly sliced

1 gallon (3.8 liters) water, heated to boiling

3 pounds (1.35kg) organic sugar

1 piece of dried bread

½ ounce (15g) dry yeast

One woman's weed is another's prized secret for myriad mystical uses—delectable sautéed greens and mixed salads and therapeutic teas as well as a very special kind of wine. Hedge witches have known for centuries that this hardy specimen can be used for calling upon helpful spirits, dispelling negative energy, and bringing good luck. One of the most important uses of this herb is divination, making this wine an absolutely enchanting way to foresee the future.

Place the flowers in a very large bowl that can handle heat; place the orange and lemon slices on top of the flowers and pour in the hot water. Cover the bowl with a clean, dry towel and place on a pantry shelf for ten days. Strain the mixture into a different bowl and spoon in the sugar, stirring to dissolve. Toast the bread and spread the yeast on top, then let it float on top of your mixture. Cover and let sit for another three days. Strain the liquid and compost the bread and any flower remains. Bottle your dandelion wine in special bottles, cork, and label it. This is a marvelous libation to share during Wiccan holidays and anytime you are in need of a positive portent.

In Vino Veritas—Visionary Wine

Marigolds are said to lend prophetic powers and more; you can make a wine using the exact same recipe for dandelion wine (see above), but make sure to pick the marigolds when the flowers have fully opened by the heat and light of the sun. Drink the marigold wine when you desire to have prophetic visions and record them. This could become part of a yearly ritual for solar new years, otherwise known as birthdays. Celebrate and commemorate these dreams and visions as vital information could come as result—after all, in wine, truth.

Thyme Tincture

Every kitchen witch's garden should be strewn with thyme, growing among the flagstones in the path, and also in the rows of herbs, filling the air with its magnificent scent and elegant beauty. You will need to keep a plentitude growing and several bunches drying in a dark corner of your pantry at all times as this plant makes a mighty fine tincture with many medicinal uses. I also suggest you start keeping clean muslin or cheesecloth, big jars, and several colored glass bottles and canning jars with lids for storing your handiwork.

    For this tincture, take one of the larger jars. Put the dried thyme in the jar and carefully pour the vinegar inside. Stir well and seal. Place on a dark shelf and shake it every day. At the end of the one month, strain through muslin. Compost the thyme residue in your garden and store the tincture in a pretty glass jar.

    Having this herbal helper around will come in handy for mouthwashes, hair rinses, ritual baths, and you can even use it to rub on achy joints and sore muscles. For a cup of thyme tea, add one teaspoon of the tincture into a cup of hot water, add a teaspoon of honey, stir, and enjoy.

1¼ cups (65g) dried thyme leaves

2 cups (480ml) apple cider vinegar

MIRACLE SALVE

Thyme in the garden attracts bees and honey made by these "thymely bees" is highly sought after. If you can come by this rarity, get as much as you can as it is redolent of Mother Nature's love and enchantment. The ancient Greeks prized this very highly, not only as a delicacy at the table, but also as a miracle salve to heal everything: the stomach, aches and pains, and even wounds. Hippocrates swore by it!

Luxuriating in Lavender

Lavender is hard not to grow, and once your seedlings and young plants have been established, they will bush out and produce loads of scented stalks, flowers, and seeds. This bounty will become your source for teas, tinctures, bath salts, and infusions. For tea, the rule of thumb is one teaspoon dried lavender flowers to one cup (240ml) boiling water to aid tummy trouble, headache, aches, insomnia, and even to help calming the mind. You can easily amp up the therapeutic power of your brew, add any of these excellent herbs—dried yarrow, St. John's wort, or chamomile.

This is a simple and streamlined way to infuse lavender: pour a heaping tablespoon into a bowl of hot water and then drape a towel over your head and breathe in the aromatic fumes to deal with respiratory issues, coughs, colds, headaches, stuffy sinuses, and nervous tension. You will come away feeling renewed and your kitchen will smell like the heavens above. You can use the water in your morning bath or add to your sink garbage disposal; grinding up the flowers refreshes that hard-duty kitchen appliance.

Lavender Tincture

Clear quart jar with lid

Dried lavender

1 cup (240ml) clear alcohol, such as vodka

2 cups (480ml) distilled water

Cheesecloth

Dark glass for storage

This cure-all should be kept on hand at all times for soothing the skin, the stomach, and anything in need of comfort. I have even seen it used to staunch bleeding in small cuts.

Fill your clear quart jar to the halfway point with the dried lavender. Pour in the alcohol also to the halfway point. Add in the water, seal securely with a lid, and shake for a few minutes until it seems well mixed. Store in a dark cupboard for one month, shaking once a day. After 30 days, strain through the cheesecloth into the dark glass storage jar and screw the lid on tightly. The lavender leavings will make lovely compost and the liquid tincture will soon prove itself indispensible in your household.

Easy Apple Cider Vinegar

This easy-peasy recipe will result in one of the most useful items in your pantry that can be used in your cookery, as a daily health drink, household cleanser, skin and facial toner, a hair rinse, and dozens of other excellent applications. Hippocrates, the founding father of Western medicine in ancient Greece, taught that he depended on two medicinal tonics, honey and vinegar. Apple cider vinegar lowers cholesterol and blood pressure and helps strengthen bones; best of all, it costs mere pennies to make as you are only using the cores and peels from the apples. Bake a couple of pies while you brew up a tonic health booster. When you add herbs to vinegar, you are enhancing the healing power of the best of both worlds.

Cut up the apple cores and peels into smaller pieces and spoon into a wide-mouthed canning jar. Pour in the water to cover the fruit, spoon in the honey, and stir well. Cover the mixture with a clean paper towel or waxed paper and place a rubber band tightly around the neck of the jar. Place on a dark shelf in your cupboard or work area and leave for two weeks. Strain the liquid and remove the compostable solids that remain, return the liquid to the jar and secure the paper and band again. Put it back on the shelf and make sure to stir daily. After one month, take a spoonful and if the acidity and flavor is to your taste, transfer to a dark bottle with sealable top. If not, wait another week and then taste it again. Vinegar will corrode metal lids so a pretty bottle with a cork is the best option.

8 organic apple cores and peels

1 quart (1 liter) water

2 tablespoons honey

✴
HERBAL ALCHEMY

The leaves and stalks of these plants are very good for making herbal vinegars: apple mint, basil, catnip, garlic mustard, orange mint, peppermint, rosemary, spearmint, thyme, and yarrow. Dill and fennel seeds work very well as do lemon and orange peels. The flowers of bee balm, chives, goldenrod, lavender, and yarrow produce a great flavor.

Roots also infuse nicely into herbal vinegars—the best are dandelion, chicory, ginger, garlic, mugwort, and burdock.

Make Your Own Herbal Vinegar

If you love everything about lavender, you may well want to create your own lavender vinegar. Many herbs make for excellent vinegars, so pay attention to which ones are especially appealing to you as you go about your gardening. The more herbs you pack into the jar, the higher the mineral content in your vinegar, which makes it more flavorful and healthy. Once you have your own apple cider vinegar or a premade organic kind you and your family love, pick an herb you know works for you and pack a quart canning jar as full as you can with it. Pour room-temperature apple cider vinegar to cover and seal with paper and bands and pop back on a dark corner shelf for six weeks, giving it a shake once a week. At the end of the infusion period, strain out any remaining compostable twigs or stems that remain, if any, and store in a colored bottle and add a pretty label. These make wonderful gifts so I recommend you get a set of labels for all your witchy brews.

Pantry Power

BLESSINGS ON A BUDGET

Instead of composting all the herbs, twigs, and stems from your brews, you can store them in a burlap or muslin sack and allow them to dry. Keep stuffing in twigs of lavender, rosemary, mint, and all the leftover plant material until you have a big bag. On a special evening, burn it in your fireplace or an outdoor bonfire and it will be like a gigantic incense burner with lovely scents wafting from the flames. And the best part? It's one hundred percent free!

Many enthusiasts enjoy several cups a day of their favorite herbal infusion, which is a large portion of herb brewed for at least four hours and as long as ten. I recommend one cup of the dried herb placed in a quart-canning jar and filled with freshly boiled water. After the steeping, strain using a non-metallic method, such as cheesecloth or bamboo. Herbal infusions can be made with the leaves and fruits that provide the magical and healing aspects of this comforting concoction. Many of the favorite kitchen witch herbs contain minerals, antioxidants, and phytochemicals. Roots, leaves, flowers, needles, and seeds can all be used—depending on which fruit or herb is chosen to be the base. There are some cases when all parts of the plant can be used in some manner, and for others only one or two parts are safe—it is important, when creating a blend from scratch, to research the ingredients to understand what parts can be used.

What do you need to attend to in your life right now? This list of herbs and associations can be your guide; one of the smartest ways to approach this methodology is to brew right before bedtime and you will awaken to a freshly infused herb. Here I've listed some of the most popular herbs and fruits used to create infusions.

* **Anise seeds and leaves** soothe cramps and aches

* **Caraway seeds** aid in romantic issues and help with colic

* **Catnip leaves** increase attractiveness

* **Chamomile flowers** help with sleep and are good for abundance

* **Dandelion leaves** make wishes come true

* **Echinacea** makes the body strong

* **Ginseng root** increases men's vigor

* **Nettle leaves** are good for lung function and hex breaking

* **Peppermint leaves** rid tummy discomfort and are cleansing

* **Pine needles** increase skin health as well as financial health

* **Rose hip fruit** is packed with Vitamin C and can halt colds and flu

* **Sage leaves** purify energy and are a natural antibiotic

* **Skullcap leaves** cures insomnia, headaches, anxiety, and nervous tension

* **St.-John's-wort leaves** act as an anti-depressant and provide protection

* **Thyme leaves** are antiseptic and a protectant

* **Yarrow flowers** reduce fever and bring courage and good luck

Merry Meet Medieval Brew

You need to start this special mixture by pouring a gallon (3.8 liters) of unfiltered sweet apple cider into a cauldron. You can buy the cider but it is even better if you make it from apples you have gathered or harvested. Take a bottle of your favorite low-cost red wine and heat gently in the pot on a low flame; add sugar, cinnamon, and cloves to your taste, but at least a tablespoon of each. Pour the cider into the warmed wine and add 13 whole cloves and 6 cinnamon sticks, then stir widdershins (counterclockwise) every six minutes. Notice how your entire home fills with the spicy sweetness of merriment. After 30 minutes, your brew should be ready to serve.

Cinnamon Liqueur

DIY ELIXIR

You can make a simple syrup, a base for any liqueur, in five short minutes by boiling 1 cup (200g) of sugar in ½ cup (120ml) of water.

You can create distinctive after-dinner drinks and digestives by adding whole herbs into simple syrup and letting them steep: try using angelica, anise, bergamot, hyssop, all mints, fennel, and, maybe the most special of all, violets. To your health!

1 cup (240ml) vodka

2 cloves

1 teaspoon ground coriander seed

1 cinnamon stick

1 cup (240ml) simple sugar syrup (see left)

This popular pagan beverage gives peppy energy and can also be a love potion. These few ingredients can lead to a lifetime of devotion.

Pour the vodka into a bowl and add the herbs. Cover with a clean, dry towel and place in a cupboard for two weeks. Strain and filter until the result is a clear liquid into which you add the simple syrup and place back on the shelf for a week. Store this in a pink- or red-capped bottle; you now have liquid love. You can add this to hot chocolate, water, tea, or milk for a delightful drink to share with a partner.

Passion Potion Spell

Lower the lamps, light red candles, and enjoy a warm cup of cocoa with a shot of the cinnamon liqueur. Speak this spell aloud as you are preparing the libation—you will radiate passion and draw your lover to you with this enchantment:

Today, I awaken the goddess in me.
By surrendering to my love for thee.
Tonight, I will heat the night with my fire.
As we drink this cup, we awaken desire.
I am alive! I am love. So mote it be.

Coming Full Circle

"I love how all-encompassing the creation of magic potions can be: you start with a handful of seeds, tend your herb garden, and end up with a pantry filled with libations that are at once medicinal, delicious, celebratory, and, most importantly, crafted with loving care."

Chapter 5

Kitchen Cupboard Cures

Centuries ago, every village depended on "medicine
women"—wise crones who used the knowledge handed
down to them as healers. They mended broken bones,
brought new babies into the world, soothed fevers, and
saved lives using the wisdom of witchery. While we live
in a modern world of cutting-edge clinics and advanced
medicine, there is still much you can do using the natural
remedies right from your pantry and kitchen garden.
The roses blooming by your front gate contain more
vitamins than the expensive bottle of chemicals on your
bathroom shelf. Your spice rack is your closest pharmacy.
Your home-brewed honey vinegar is a powerful tonic
your family will love. Inside your cupboard, a whole
magical world awaits with which you can conjure much
health and happiness.

The Homely Healing Arts

I began practicing the craft as a child. For me, witchcraft was and is the most natural thing in the world—and indeed it is all about being in the natural world. On woodland walks, my Aunt Edith pointed out nettles, wild mint, Queen Anne's lace, and other herbs that grew by creek beds near my home. We picked, steeped, and sipped concoctions we made together as she imparted her homely wisdom. Little did I know at the time that I was being gently schooled as an apprentice kitchen witch.

Lately, I have been called upon to craft spells for peace of mind; so many of us are overwhelmed due to the fragmented lifestyles requiring long hours at work, zillions of e-mails, text messages, social media, and all the other demands that don't stop flooding in. Yet how often do you see a stressed-out witch? Rarely, I assure you.

We witches also have to keep pace with the modern world, but our connection to the earth and the cycles of nature helps maintain balance and harmony, despite the hurly burly of these tech-driven times. This chapter is aimed at conjuring wellness so you can stay centered, grounded, and healthy. When our grandmothers and elders who came before us tended cuts, bruises, colds, fevers, and other illnesses their families suffered, they didn't have a corner drugstore. Instead, these wise women relied on simple wisdom, common sense, and pantries well stocked with herbal remedies. These preparations were made from plants that grew in the kitchen garden or from wild weeds gathered in the fields and woods surrounding their homes. This collection of kitchen-cupboard cures combines the wisdom of our elders with a modern kitchen witch's sensibilities. Yes, you will save money but, more importantly, you will begin to learn what works for you and master the art of self-care as you bring much comfort to your loved ones. Here are tips and kitchen-witch secrets to healing many maladies and feeling your best every day, come rain or shine.

Lavender Space-Clearing Spell

To do any healing work, you must first clear clutter, both physical and otherwise, that creates energy blocks. Banish "stale" and unhealthy energy from your kitchen workspace and living space with this herbal magic. Steep lavender in hot water; once the infusion has cooled to room temperature, dip your fingertips in it and sprinkle tiny droplets throughout your home while intoning these words:

All is new here now, I say.
Make way, be gone, goodbye
All here is new, say I.
So mote it be!

Use the remainder of the lavender infusion to wash your front steps or stoop—the entry to your sanctuary—thereby clearing and cleansing the threshold of your home.

You will notice that every time you enter your home, it feels lighter and brighter thanks to the energetic de-cluttering.

The Spice Rack of Life

Did you know your pantry is like a pharmacy? Thankfully, it is far cheaper.

* **Cayenne** promotes circulation and boosts metabolism.

* **Turmeric** is an immune champion and boosts production of antioxidants and reduction of inflammation. Some centenarians have credited their long, healthy lives to drinking turmeric-root tea daily.

* **Cumin** is loaded with phytochemicals, antioxidants, iron, copper, calcium, potassium, manganese, selenium, zinc, and magnesium, and contains high amounts of B-complex. It also helps with insomnia.

* **Cilantro** (coriander) is a good source of iron, magnesium, phytonutrients, and flavonoids, and is also high in dietary fiber. Cilantro has been used for thousands of years as a digestive, helping lower blood sugar as it has hypoglycemic properties, possibly the result of helping to stimulate insulin secretion.

* **Parsley** is a nutrient-rich and detoxifying herb and acts as anti-inflammatory and anti-spasmodic, helping conditions from colic to indigestion. Rub it on itchy skin for instant relief.

* **Sage** is very beneficial in treating gum and throat infections. Sage tea has helped ease depression and anxiety for generations.

* **Ginger** stimulates circulation and is an excellent digestive, aiding in absorption of food and minimizing bloat.

* **Cinnamon** is a power spice. Just a half-teaspoon a day can dramatically reduce blood glucose levels in those with type 2 diabetes and help lower cholesterol.

* **Thyme** is a cure for hangover and doubles to alleviate colds and bronchitis.

* **Clove** is an antifungal and alleviates toothaches.

Pack your pantry with these seasonings for optimal health and happiness.

Breathe Easy Spell

Banish colds and coughs or keep them at bay with this sweet-smelling spell. In a blue bottle, shake together the following essential oils:

10 drops rosemary
10 drops tea tree
10 drops eucalyptus
10 drops lavender
1 teaspoon sea salt

Hold the open container in both hands under your nose and breathe in deeply three times. After the last exhalation, intone:

Power of wind,
Strength of the trees,
Energy of the earth,
Salts of the sea,
I call upon you to keep me well and strong.
With harm to none, so mote it be.

You can administer this respiratory booster with four drops added to the water of a vaporizer or diffuser or a cotton ball tucked into your pillowcase. Six drops poured into the running water of a hot bath will ease breathing immediately.

ESSENTIAL OILS FOR COMMON AILMENTS

Use these oils in bath water, diffusers, dabbed onto pulse points, or sprays to infuse your home with the healing vitality of these plant essences.

Allergies: chamomile, melissa

Headaches: geranium, lavender, linden, peppermint

Immune boosters: hyssop, jasmine, rose, thyme

Insomnia: clary sage, hops, lavender

Colds and flu: eucalyptus, lavender, pine, thyme

Tummy troubles: basil, chamomile, peppermint

Cramps: linden, sunflower, yarrow

Arthritis: eucalyptus, marjoram, pine, rosemary

Fatigue: bergamot, clary sage, neroli, rose

Dandy Sassafras Ginger Detox

❋ DECOCTIONS 101

Roots, bark, and herbs with tough stems and seeds don't really lend themselves to the method of infusing. Decocting is boiling and then evaporating by simmering slowly to produce the most concentrated liquid, which is excellent in medicines. Use a coffee grinder for roots and small pieces of bark and stems to make quick work of these. I recommend the decoction method for the roots of willow, sarsaparilla, wild cherry, yohimbe, yucca, licorice, parsley, dandelion, angelica, and cohosh.

When I was little, living on the family farm, I accompanied my part-Cherokee dad to the woods, looking for sassafras roots to make tea. I loved the taste; it was delightful and also gave me more energy. After apprenticing with my dad for a few years, he allowed me to go out alone, gathering the source of my dearly beloved beverage. Years later, I discovered that sassafras was highly prized by Native Americans who used it for medicine and who were extremely knowledgeable about combining herbs to amplify their power.

This morning-medicine is inspired by a shamanic native-healing recipe using sassafras roots, dandelion greens, and slices of wild ginger. For a wonderfully medicinal decoction, take a half-cup of each and boil them in spring water. After steeping for 12 minutes, stir in honey and enjoy. It is pleasantly surprising how good the detox tastes and even more how the herbs combine to eliminate toxins from the body, chiefly the kidney and liver. During the holidays or pagan-feast times, we all imbibe and enjoy rich foods, good wine, and sugary desserts. This purifying herbal blend will cleanse the organs that cleanse your body, thus aiding wellness. This detox should be used seasonally and is not intended for daily use, due to its great power.

Oxymel—An Ancient Tonic

Oxymel is a very old-fashioned tonic that dates back to ancient times and that has fallen out of fashion. It remains a favorite of herbal healers and is made of two seemingly opposing ingredients—honey and vinegar. Herbs can be added to great effect and when you see honey-menthol cough drops on the pharmacy shelf, note their 2,000-year-old origins. Oxymels are supremely effective for respiratory issues. The recipe is simplicity itself, equal parts honey and vinegar poured over herbs in a canning jar. Store in a dark cupboard and give the sealed jar a good shake every day. After two weeks, strain out the herbs through cheesecloth and store in the fridge.

HERBS FOR OXYMELS

The herbs that I would recommend using for this healing tonic are oregano, elder flower, sage, balm, mint, lemon peel, thyme, lavender, rose petals, hyssop, and fennel.

Blackberries—Roadside Medicine

Blackberries are one of life's sweetest gifts, growing abundantly in the bramble along many a rambling path. An extremely effective medicinal tonic can be made by soaking 4 cups (520g) of berries in a quart (1 liter) of malt vinegar for three days. Drain and strain the liquid into a pan. Simmer and stir in sugar, 2¼ cups (450g) to every 2 cups (475ml) of tonic. Boil gently for 5 minutes and skim off any foam. Cool and pour into a sealable jar.

This potion is so powerful that you can add a teaspoon into a cup of water and cure tummy aches, cramps, fevers, coughs, and colds. Best of all, blackberry vinegar is both a medicine and a highly prized culinary flavoring for sauces and salads. Pour some over your apple pie and cream and you will soon scurry off to pick blackberries all summer.

Comfrey Comfort

Comfrey is beloved by kitchen witches and is one of the best-known healing herbs of all times. It has even been referred to as "a one-herb pharmacy" for its inherent curative powers. Well known and widely used by early Greeks and Romans, its botanical name, *symphytum*, from the Greek *symphyo*, means to "make grow together," referring to its traditional use of healing fractures. Comfrey relieves pain and inflammation. Comfrey salve will be a mainstay of your home first-aid kit. Use it on cuts, scrapes, rashes, sunburn, and almost any skin irritation. Comfrey salve can also bring comfort to aching arthritic joints and sore muscles.

Lavender Comfrey Cure-All Salve

¾ cup (180ml) comfrey-infused oil

¼ cup (60ml) coconut oil

4 tablespoons beeswax

10 drops lavender essential oil

Combine the comfrey and coconut oils. Heat the oil and wax together until the wax melts completely. Pour into a clean, dry jar. When the mixture has cooled a little, but not yet set, add 10 drops of lavender essential oil, which is also an antiseptic. Stir it through. Seal the jar and store in a cabinet to use anytime you scratch yourself working in the garden or want to renew and soften your hands and feet after a lot of house and yard work. One note, use it on the outside of your skin and it will work wonders, but if a cut is deep, don't get it inside the wound. Let your physician handle that. Comfrey is a miracle plant for healing; in combination with the lavender, this power duo will restore your spirit along with your skin.

Heart's Ease Cauldron Cure

Here is a soothing sip that can uplift your spirits anytime and also serves to ward off chills. This combination of herbs brings about the "letting go" of sorrows, worries, and doubts, and reignites feelings of self-love.

Stir all the ingredients together in a clean cauldron to mix. Pour into a colored jar, and seal the lid tightly. When you are ready to brew, pour hot water over the herbs, two teaspoons per cup. While this steeps for 5 minutes, write down on a small piece of paper any thoughts or fears of which you need to rid yourself. Now say each one aloud, then chant, "Begone!" After this letting-go ritual, burn the paper together with sage in the cauldron on your altar. As you sip the tea, enjoy your renewed sense of self and peace of mind.

1 ounce (28g) dried rosehips
1 ounce (28g) dried hibiscus
2 ounces (56g) dried mint
1 tablespoon dried ginger root

✳ MOTHER NATURE'S MULTIVITAMIN

Once a rose has bloomed and all petals have fallen away, the hip is ready to be picked. Ground rose hips are the best source of immune-boosting Vitamin C; they contain 50 percent more Vitamin C than oranges. One tablespoon provides more than the recommended daily adult allowance of 90 mg for men and 75 mg for women. The pulp from rose hips may be used in sauces or made into jelly. What a delicious way to ward off colds and ailments!

Handmade Herbal Amulet

You will experience years of enjoyment from tending your garden, as Voltaire taught us in his masterpiece, *Candide*. You can share that pleasure with your friends and those you love with gifts from your garden. Your good intentions will be returned many times over. I keep a stock of small muslin drawstring bags for creating amulets. If you are a crafty kitchen witch, you can make the bags, sewing them by hand, and stuff the dried herbs inside.

Amulets should be kept on your person at all times, in a pocket, in your purse or book bag, or on a string around your neck.

* **For courage and heart:** mullein or borage

* **For good cheer:** nettle or yarrow

* **For fellow witches:** ivy, broomstraw, maidenhair fern

* **For safe travels:** comfrey

* **For fertility:** cyclamen or mistletoe

* **For protection from deceit:** snapdragon

* **For good health:** rue

* **For success:** woodruff

* **For strength:** mugwort

* **For youthful looks:** an acorn

Conjuring by the Cup

Tea is not only a delectable drink, but also of equal importance are the great healing powers contained in each cup. Growing and drying herbs for your own kitchen-witchery brews is truly one of life's simple pleasures. Tea conjures a very powerful alchemy because, when you drink it, you take the magic inside of you. For an ambrosial brew with the power to calm any storm, add a sliver of ginger root and a teaspoon each of chamomile and peppermint to two cups of boiling water. Let steep and, as the mixture brews and cools, pray using the words on the right.

This day I pray for strength and health,
And the wisdom to see the beauty in each waking moment.
Blessings abound; good health is true wealth.

Green Witchery Healthy Brews

Herbal tea nourishes the soul, heals the body, and calms the mind. Try any of the following:

* **Blackberry leaf tea** reduces mood swings, evens glucose levels, thus aiding weight management. This miraculous herbal even helps circulation and aids such issues as inflammation and varicose veins. It is helpful to cancer patients and is believed to be a preventative.

* **Catnip** is one of the witchiest of teas and is not only grown as fun for your feline familiar. At the first inkling of a sore throat or impending cold, drink a warm cup of catnip tea and head off to bed. You will awaken feeling much better. Catnip soothes the nervous system and can safely help get a restless child go off to sleep as it's a gentle but potent sleep-inducer.

* **Cardamom** is a favorite of expectant mothers everywhere as it calms nausea and morning sickness; this east-India fragrant is excellent for digestion, clears and cleans your mouth and throat. Anyone who likes cinnamon will love cardamom.

* **Nettle** raises your energy level, boosts the immune system, and is packed with iron and vitamins.

* **Fennel** is excellent for awakening and uplifting and is great for digestion and cleansing. Fennel also is a natural breath freshener.

* **Echinacea** lends an increased and consistent sense of well-being and prevents colds and flu. It is a very powerful immune booster.

* **Ginger root** calms and cheers while aiding digestion and nausea and can also fend off coughs and sore throats.

* **Dandelion root** grounds and centers, providing many minerals and nutrients. This wonderful weed is also a cleanser and a wholly natural detoxifier.

Sacred Self-Care 101

The pace of life today can cause enormous strain and anxiety. Not only does this pressure and strain get in the way of the fun of life, it also affects your health. The "way of the witch" never lets worry get in the way of wellness, and these soothing spells and relaxing rites will add greatly to your quality of life.

Simple Salt Magic

The one thing every household has in the kitchen is salt, either plain white grains or the larger, kosher crystals. This most common of cupboard condiments is also an essential in magic, dating back thousands of years and used by Egyptians, Chaldeans, Babylonians, and early European tribes for purification, protection, and cleansing. Salt is often utilized in hoodoo, sprinkled on doorsteps and pathways to keep bad spirits away (as well as bad people), and added into witch bottles to clear energy. During the era of the early Roman Empire, soldiers were paid in salt—it was that valuable. Long have these grains been used to preserve and improve the taste of foods. Perhaps the highest purpose of salt is as a healer; it is essential in the diet for good health and external uses in baths and rubs can be enormously relaxing. Salt removes negative energy and can vanquish a headache in short order with the following magical application.

Headache Healer—Salt Serenity Spell

Fill a tea kettle and set it to boil. Pour hot water into a mug and add a full tablespoon of salt. Once it has cooled to a warm temperature, hold the mug against each of your temples in turn and keep it there for a long moment. Dip your forefinger of your left hand into the salt water and gently rub each of your temples and your forehead in circular movements. Sit or lay flat in silence for some time with your eyes closed. If this turns into a nap, all the better. When you are ready, rise and your headache will be at bay. Place the cup on your kitchen altar for a period of 24 hours so it can draw out any negative energy from your home. The following day, throw the salt water from the cup onto your front step or sidewalk to keep any bad juju away. As you walk down your front path, you'll notice that you feel clear-headed and peaceful.

Setting Sun Spell

The jar of bay leaf in your spice cupboard will get you one step closer to tranquility. To clear energy and prepare for a week of calm clarity, find your favorite white flower—iris, lily, rose, one that is truly beautiful to your eye. Monday's setting sun is the time for this spell, immediately after the sun goes below the horizon. Anoint a white candle with jasmine oil and place on your altar. Take your single white blossom and add that to your altar in a bowl of freshly drawn water. Place a whole bay leaf on a glass dish in front of the lit candle and speak aloud the words of the spell on the right.

Burn the bay leaf in the fire of the candle and put it in the glass dish where it can turn into ash, smudging as it burns.

This fire is pure; this flower is holy;
this water is clear.
These elements purify me.
I walk in light with nothing in my way.
My energy is pure, my spirit is holy,
my being is clear.
Blessed be.

Bay Leaf Balm

Any body oil or herbal oil can be turned into a salve with the addition of wax. The ratio for a body salve is 3 ounces (90ml) coconut oil to 1 ounce (30ml) beeswax. If you have a bay laurel tree, pick some fresh leaves. You can also go to your spice rack and take three leaves from the jar and grind them in your mortar and pestle until broken up into fine, little pieces. Set aside a fourth whole leaf. Use a double boiler to heat the oil and wax until completely melted. Test the viscosity of your salve by pouring a dab onto a cold plate. If satisfied with the consistency, pour off into clean jars to cool. If you need to add more wax, now is the time to do it. Balms are simply salves with the addition of essential oils. Add two drops of eucalyptus essential oil and two drops of lemon oil while the mix is still warm. Sprinkle in the finely crushed bay laurel, stir well, and seal to preserve the aroma.

Bay leaf balm will have a wonderfully calming effect anytime you use it and can be rubbed on your temples when you need to de-stress. I recommend Sunday night soaks, where you slather on the balm before stepping into a hot bath. Take a washcloth and massage your skin, then lie back and relax for 20 minutes. When you drain the bathtub, your stress will also empty out, and you can start your week afresh, ready to handle anything that comes your way.

Body Purification Ritual Bath

Since the time of the ancients in the Mediterranean and Mesopotamia, salts of the sea combined with soothing oils have been used to purify the body by way of gentle, ritualized rubs. From Bathsheba to Cleopatra, these natural salts have been used to smooth the skin and enhance circulation, which is vital to overall physical health as skin is the single largest organ in the human body. Dead Sea salts have long been a popular export and are readily available at most health food shops and spas. You can make your own salts, however, and not only control the quality and customize the scent, but save money, too. The definitive benefit that is far above the cost savings is that you can imbue your concoction with your intention, which is absolutely imperative when you are performing rites of self-healing,

Shekinah's Garden of Eden Salts

Shekinah translates to "She who dwells within" and is the Hebrew name for the female aspect of God. Olden legend has it that she co-created the world side by side with Yahweh, the god of Israel. This simple recipe recalls the scents and primal memories of that edenic paradise.

Mix well and store in a colored and well-capped glass bottle. Prepare for the ritual rub by lighting citrus- and rose-scented candles. Step out of your clothes and hold the salts in the palms of your hand. Pray aloud:

3 cups (385g) Epsom salts

½ cup (120ml) sweet almond oil

1 tablespoon glycerin

4 drops ylang-ylang essential oil

2 drops jasmine essential oil

Shekinah, may your wisdom guide me,
My body is a temple to you.
Here I worship today, with heart
and hands,
Body and soul.
I call upon you for healing,
Shekinah, bring me breath and life.
Ancient one, I thank you
With heart and hands,
Body and soul.

Use these salts with a clean washcloth or new sponge and gently scrub your body while standing in the shower or bathtub. The ideal time is during a waxing morning moon or at midnight during a new moon. You will glow with health and inner peace.

Saffron Serenity Spell

This evening ritual is a wonderful way to end the day. Light a yellow candle for mental clarity, and anoint it with calming and uplifting bergamot oil. Place a yellow rose in a vase to the left of the candle. To the right, place a bowl containing at least two citrine or quartz crystals.

Saffron water is made by boiling a single teaspoon of saffron from your cupboard in 2 quarts (2 liters) of distilled water. Let cool to room temperature and pour into the bowl of crystals. Put your hands together as in prayer and dip your hands in the bowl. Touch your third eye in the center of your forehead, anointing yourself with the saffron water. Now, speak aloud:

Goddess great, fill me with your presence
This night, I am whole and at peace.
Breathing in, breathing out,
I feel your safe embrace.
And so it is.

The Serenity Spectrum

I have already explained how powerful candles can be (see page 32), but did you know you can burn colored candles on certain days of the week for all kinds of well-being? The guide below shows which candles to use and when.

* For inner peace, burn **silver** candles on **Monday**.

* To let go of anger, burn **orange** candles on **Tuesday**.

* For mental clarity, burn **yellow** candles on **Wednesday**.

* For a peaceful home, burn **blue** candles on **Thursday**.

* For kindness and compassion, burn **pink** candles on **Friday**.

* For success at work and for physical well-being, burn **green** candles on **Friday**.

* To overcome regret or guilt, burn **white** candles on **Saturday**.

* For self-confidence and to overcome fear, burn **red** candles on **Sunday**.

Coming Full Circle

"Every day, you can renew your own health and wellness in many small ways; a cup of green tea with a morning prayer can be a simple rite that gives you calm and greater wellness."

 Chapter 6

The Kitchen Witch's Garden

Gardening is one of the most creative things you can do
and an exercise in mindfulness. It keeps you grounded
with a deep connection to the earth. Growing herbs to use
in remedies and spellcraft is doubly rewarding;
with each passing season, you will grow in your wisdom
and skill. Your garden—whether it is a balcony full of
blooms or a plot out back—can be a sanctuary, a place
where your spirit is renewed and restored. Tending and
growing these magical herbs and potent plants is a kind
of botanical alchemy; the teas, tinctures, potions, recipes,
and flower essences you craft are proof that yours is an
enchanted garden.

Supernatural Seeds and Herbs of Happiness

I have lived in homes where my only gardening options were containers on a deck or planters on the front stoop. This taught me that you can do a lot with seed packets, pots, and an open mind. When selecting space for your kitchen witchery garden you can have something as simple as a set of containers; this can be planned as with any other garden space. If you are lucky to have a backyard or land, I suggest you begin the designing process by incorporating all the plants you know and want to use in your magical workings and your cookery, and always allow yourself to experiment. Trying veggies or seeds that are new to you can be enormously rewarding. I agree with Londoner Alys Fowler, who is one of Britain's top gardeners. She says there is no earthly reason why roses and cabbages can't go side by side, and veggies can nicely nestle in among flowers. Once you have tried a few such painterly plantings, you can give yourself a free hand in your creative approach.

A witch's garden should have an aspect of wildness to it. Let the alyssum reseed itself and spread all over, creating a carpet of beauty. Allow the morning glory, jasmine, and nasturtiums to climb the fence with abandon. I encourage you to experiment and grow anything your heart desires. As the seasons pass, your garden will reflect your self-growth and will also be a haven you turn to for reflection.

Your Magical Intent

Do you use chamomile regularly? Do you purify your space with sage? Are rosemary, mint, and lavender favorites in your sachets and teas? Think of all the herbs and plants you love and use often, then begin researching their upkeep and care. Make sure to research your planting zone so you get the optimal climate to nurture your plants and herbs. Once you have planned your plantings, infuse your plot with magical intention. Keep careful track of your progress in your Book of Shadows. As you grow in experience and expertise, so will the healing power of your plot.

Remember to research plants and herbs that can be toxic or poisonous to ensure the safety of children or our canine and feline friends. Many a beloved power flower handed down to us is excellent for magical workings but not at all appropriate for tea, edibles, or such things. Make sure visiting children stay far away from wisteria, rhododendron, lily of the valley, narcissus, foxglove, larkspur, hydrangea, and oleander. They are beautiful but deadly, literally.

Every new moon is an opportunity to sow seeds for new beginnings and deepen your magical intent. Your plantings can be a tool you use for a better life, bringing brighter health and greater abundance, as well as mindfulness and serenity. Nature is our greatest teacher and a garden is a gift through which you both give and receive.

A Garden of Health and Healing

Herein, I have gathered the plants, flowers, and herbs that will prove most useful in your kitchen witchery. Most are hardy plants that you and your circle will enjoy for many long years to come and that will bring both beauty and power to your garden.

Thyme—An Herb for the Ages

You could say that thyme is a classic herb, so much so that the venerable Virgil and Pliny sang the praises of this medicinal mint relative over 2,000 years ago. While thyme loves Mediterranean weather, it can grow elsewhere from seeds and cuttings. Good for the stomach and especially effective for respiratory relief, thyme induces sweats to remove toxins and reduce fever. Thyme honey tea is truly a sweet way to make the medicine go down, so much so that you will drink it even when hale and hearty. Thyme is also a culinary plant, making

a delightful additive to savory dishes. When I lived in warmer climes, I planted wooly thyme among the flagstones of my front yard and let it spread as much as possible. When I came home from work, the sunny, 80-plus-degree weather had warmed the thyme, creating a perfumed walkway. Arriving home was a heavenly experience.

It has been believed for centuries that thyme brings courage and both inner and physical strength. Even when you are facing seemingly insurmountable odds, spells and smudging featuring thyme can get you on track and bring you to your goal. I think the greatest of all aspects of thyme is to rid your home and family of melancholy and overcome despair after extreme difficulty and loss. If your loved ones have experienced a catastrophe, try thyme for rituals of magic and restitution. I have no doubt that practitioners of green witchery will be singing the praises of thyme for at least 2,000 more years.

✳

DREAM THYME

I gather and dry thyme to use in sachets so the divine fragrance freshens linens and laundry. A little bag of this dried thyme tucked in your pillowcase makes for sweeter sleep. As if all that wasn't enough, it also repels bugs and pests but attracts honeybees!

Balm for All Sorrows

Lemon balm also goes by the equally lovely Latinate *Melissa*. From Greco-Roman times, this relative of the mint family has been held as a significant medicine. You can grow lemon balm with ease from seed packets in almost any kind of soil, but it likes shade in the afternoon to prevent wilting. This is one of the happy plants that will "volunteer" and spread in your garden and can be used in love magic—to bring love to you and also heal after a break up or divorce. It can also be employed as an aphrodisiac.

Infusions and teas made from lemon balm make good on the offer the name implies—it can soothe the heart and any lingering upset, blue moods, and aches and pains from trauma, both physical and emotional. We should all grow as much as possible and let some of it go to seed for those new plants that will pop up in unexpected places in your herb garden. A kitchen witch never complains about a plentitude of balm; anyone who makes much use of lemon balm in brews and cookery will enjoy an abundance of love.

Chives for Good Cheer

Allium, also known as chives, is a blessedly easy plant to grow anywhere and everywhere—on the kitchen windowsill or in a garden patch. A member of the onion family, this is a lovely case where the entire plant—bulb, leaves, and flowers—can be eaten. Plant the bulbs 6 inches (15 cm) apart, water, and you can pretty much ignore them after as all they require is water. A plus is that this relative of the onion has insect-repellant properties, so you can plant rows of this beside veggies and fruits and the bugs will stay away. Allium propagates quickly, so you can dig up mature bulbs and separate them and replant. One tip to remember is that chives do lose their flavor when dried, so use them fresh.

The flowers are a lovely surprise to add to salads for their edible beauty and many a kitchen witch uses chives in all manner of dishes as it is good for weight management and is a plant of protection for both home and garden. Chives were used by practitioners of old in amulets to ward off evil spirits and mischievous fairy folk. Freshly cut bunches were also hung beside the sickbed to speed healing, especially for children. If you see a home surrounded by rows of allium, you know its occupants hold to the "old ways."

Basil—Bounty and Beauty

This sweet-tasting herb is excellent in savory dishes. Basil truly grows like a weed and you should cultivate it right on the kitchen windowsill so you can snip and add to your Italian-inspired dishes. Give your basil plants plenty of sun, lots of water, and you will reap a mighty bounty to share with the neighbors. Old wives and hedge witches claim that basil protects your home while it also brings prosperity and happiness. Basil helps steady the mind, brings love, peace, and money, and protects against insanity—what more can you want? Basil has many practical magical applications such as making peace after disagreements. The benefits of this plant are as plentiful as the plant itself; it can be used in attracting and getting love and, on the highest vibrational level, abetting psychic abilities, even astral projection.

Basil Money Magic

Harvest several leaves from your basil plants and place them inside a clear bowl of water on your kitchen altar overnight. In the morning, remove the leaves and let them dry on your kitchen windowsill. Touch the water to your fingertips and touch your purse, wallet, and anywhere you keep money. If you handle money at your workplace, bottle some of the basil water in a tiny jar and do the same. Once the soaked leaves have dried, place one in your wallet, purse, and pockets to attract money to you and yours. It also repels thieves and protects from a loss of wealth. You can also put some basil leaves on your desk at home or work to enhance prosperity for your employer or before asking for a raise. Basil is truly a kitchen witch's boon.

EDIBLE FLOWERS

Organic, pesticide-free posies are tasty additions to salads, cake décor, and even savories, such as fried squash blossom. Flowers add a stunning beauty to any dish. Grab your basket and add a bouquet to your culinary creations: impatiens, marigold, gladiola, daylily, cornflower, daisy, carnation, and viola. My favorites are peppery, fresh-flavored nasturtiums, which are so easy to grow and the yellow, red and, bright-orange blooms are the colors of happiness.

Daisy and Echinacea

This faithful flower's name is derived from the Anglo-Saxon *dæges eage*, "day's eye," since it closes in the evening. The daisy has been used in one of the oldest of love charms. To know if your true love is returned, take a daisy and intone, "He loves me, he loves me not" until the last petal is plucked and the answer will be revealed. This flower is not just a boon for romance, however, it is also useful in herbal medicine for aches, bruises, wounds, inflammation, and soothing eye baths. As a flower remedy, it is quite good to help with exhaustion and is a highly regarded cure in homeopathy.

Echinacea is a member of the daisy family that has become wildly popular as a healer for colds and as a powerful immune booster, increasing your T-cell count and fighting off illnesses both minor and major. Echinacea is an herb of abundance, attracting more prosperity, but it can be used in magic workings to amplify the power of spellwork.

Rosemary for Remembrance

Rosemary is another of the herbs that thrives best in warm, Mediterranean climes but can also weather the cold. Tough to grow from seed, cuttings are an easier way to start your row of rosemary plants in your garden. Pots of this bushy plant can enjoy spring and summer and come in from the cold to a sheltered porch or by a sunny window when temperatures drop. As a bonus, it requires little water. Rosemary is fantastic as a seasoning for potatoes, roast chicken, and makes any Sunday supper taste better and brighter. You can pinch off the aromatic needles to dress plates or sprinkle into

soups and stews. Beyond enhancing your cookery, this is a primary plant for rejuvenation and is prized for how it helps restore after lingering illness; elixirs and essential oils made from rosemary stimulate and energize as they comfort. In Greco-Roman times, rosemary was believed to help the memory. An excellent kitchen witchery practice is to take dried or fresh rosemary and add it to a steam for an easy infusion, where it aids breathing, muscle aches, and anxiety. You can accomplish the same by adding rosemary to a hot bath. Lie back and relax, remembering happy times in your life, and those that lie right ahead of you.

Coltsfoot—Dispeller of Coughs

Coltsfoot, also called butterbur, is so named for the leaf's resemblance to a horse's hoof. Viewed as a weed except for those who know, this spiky, flowering plant grows wild along creeks, wetlands, or loamy fields. *Tussilago*, the Latinate botanical name, means cough dispeller, and this is a powerful aid to those with asthma or bronchial conditions and is also very good medicine for colds and flu. In folklore, young maidens would use the leaves in a simple spell to see their future husband in the distance, galloping toward them. Truly knowledgeable hedge witches have a herd of coltsfoot in the shadiest, dampest part of their property.

Angelica—Heavenly Guardian Flower

Angelica, said to bloom first on Archangel Michael's name day, is part of the carrot family and is a tall, hollow-stemmed plant with umbrella-shaped clusters of pale, white flowers, tinged with green. Candying the stalks in sugar was an old-fashioned favorite; it was also traditionally used to cure colds and relieve coughs. Nowadays, seeds are used to make chartreuse, a digestif and uniquely tasty liqueur. This guardian flower is a protector, as one might expect from a plant associated with archangels, and is used to reverse curses, break hexes, and fend off negative energies. Drying and curing the root makes for a traditional talisman, which can be carried in your pocket or in an amulet to bring long life. Many a wise woman has used angelica leaves in baths and spellwork to rid a household of dark spirits. If the bad energy is intense, burn the angelica leaves with frankincense to exorcise them from your space. While you are protecting yourself and your home from negativity during this angelica smudging session, you will also experience heightened psychism. Pay close attention to your dreams after this; important messages will come through.

Lavender is Love

Lavender is blessedly easy to grow as it is a shrubby plant of Mediterranean origins. It is prized for its lovely scent and is a powerful healing plant with other properties, and can be used for making teas, tisanes, being infused into honey, and has many more practical uses. It can even prosper in dry and droughty areas, so make sure your kitchen garden has at least one of the hardy varieties so you can dry bundles to use in your spellwork as well as in your recipes.

Lavender Self-Blessing Ritual

The time you take to restore yourself is precious. Morning is the optimal time to perform a self-blessing, which will help you maintain your physical health and provide an emotional boost each and every day. Take a bundle of dried lavender grown in your kitchen garden or from a purveyor of organic herbs and place it into a muslin sack. Knead the lavender three times and breathe in the calming scent. Beginning at the top of your head, your crown chakra, pass the pouch all the way down to your feet, gently touching your other six sacred chakras: your forehead, throat, solar plexus, upper and lower abdomen, and pelvis. Holding the lavender bag over your heart, speak aloud the spell on the right.

Gone are sorrows, illness, and woe;
Here wisdom and health flows.
My heart is whole, joy fills my soul.
Blessed be me.

Sage Wisdom

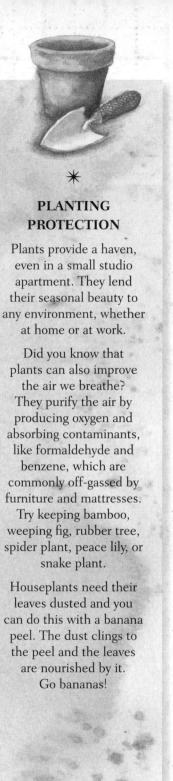

Every kitchen witch should grow a pot of sage or a big patch in her garden. Sage is a must to have on hand for clearing energy. It also increases psychic potential. Most kitchen witches are highly imaginative and very inventive folk. Whether your passion is growing an artful garden, throwing pots, cookery, or music, you can stay in better touch with your personal muse. Call her to you anytime, day or night, by your own design. This is especially important if you are feeling uninspired or struggling with a bout of writer's block.

Head out to your garden or the sunny spot on the deck where your hardiest sage grows. Take three large and extra-long sticks of your favorite incense and bind strands of sage around the incense with purple thread. Tie it off and you have a sage wand. Before any creative endeavor, you can light this wand and wave it around your workspace, filling the area with inspiration. Close your eyes and meditate upon the work you will begin. You have cleared your space, invited the muse, and your work will be superb, worthy of notice from the gods and goddesses.

PLANTING PROTECTION

Plants provide a haven, even in a small studio apartment. They lend their seasonal beauty to any environment, whether at home or at work.

Did you know that plants can also improve the air we breathe? They purify the air by producing oxygen and absorbing contaminants, like formaldehyde and benzene, which are commonly off-gassed by furniture and mattresses. Try keeping bamboo, weeping fig, rubber tree, spider plant, peace lily, or snake plant.

Houseplants need their leaves dusted and you can do this with a banana peel. The dust clings to the peel and the leaves are nourished by it. Go bananas!

Aloe—Medicine Tree

One of Mother Nature's most effective healers is aloe. When I lived in colder areas of frost and snow, I grew aloe in a wide pot with good drainage and placed it in the sunniest spot in the kitchen, where it thrived with very little water. I am truly fortunate to live today where it never gets below freezing, so I have a towering aloe in the left garden corner that is growing to tree-like proportion. When anyone in the household gets a burn, a bug bite, a rash, a scratch, an itch, or sunburn, I march back and grab a stem and apply the juice liberally to the affected area. We use it as a medicine and as a beauty application for facials, hair gel, skin massage, and feel so blessed that all this heavenly healing is utterly free of cost. Aloe propagates through baby plants sprouting off the sides, which you can repot into little clay containers and give as kitchen witchery gifts to your circle to share the healing energy as well as protection and luck, a deterrent to loneliness and to help abet success. Grow in the home to provide protection from household accidents. Burn on the night of a full moon to bring a new lover by the new moon.

Mint—Refresh Your Mental Powers

Another useful herb is mint, which is so easily grown that a little bunch in the backyard can go on to become a scented, attractive groundcover. It is also called the flower of eternal refreshment. Woven into a laurel, it bestows brilliance, artistic inspiration, and prophetic ability. As a tea, it accomplishes miracles of calming the stomach and the mind at the same time.

A Gardener's Grimoire— Spells and Secrets

Garden spells are among the most satisfying aspects of the craft; you will feel closer to the lineage of the wise women who came before you. This is earth magic, pure and simple. The charms and enchantments that follow will grow your witchery skills as quickly as the plants in your plot.

Wish Upon a Waxing Moon

This spell will sanctify your garden space. When the moon is waxing, growing larger toward the phase of fullness, gather green and purple candles and anoint them with sandalwood and rose oil, respectively. To create a simple outdoor altar, place the candles on a large, flat rock or your garden wall. Place a small, potted ivy vine on the altar, along with a cup of water. Burn sandalwood incense on the northern side of your outdoor altar. Now close your eyes and meditate upon your hopes and dreams of growth—personal, business, spiritual, for loved ones. When the incense has almost completely burned, take the ivy and plant it in the optimal spot in your garden, where it can thrive and spread, creating beauty as it vines on a wall or fence. Use the cup to water the plant. Now bow and pray, using the words on the right.

This ivy is now a botanical "familiar" and as it flourishes, so will you. I encourage you to continually revitalize your outdoor altar by adorning it with sacred objects that have meaning to you: iridescent feathers, a lovely rock from a nearby creek, a bright red pomegranate, a perfect white rose, or anything else you find in nature that will make a perfect offering.

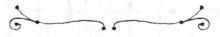

As this living thing expands,
So shall the power of this magical space grow.
Oh, goddess of the Earth, I dedicate my magic to you.
Harm to none and only good work from this holy space.

New Moon Ritual—Sowing Seeds of Change

Nature is the ultimate creator. From a nearby gardening or hardware store, get an assortment of seed packets to plant newness into your life. If your thumb is not the greenest, try nasturtiums, which are extremely hardy, grow quickly, and spread, beautifying any area. They re-seed themselves, which is a lovely bonus.

On a new-moon morning, draw a square in your yard with a "found-in-nature" wand—a fallen branch. Apartment dwellers can use a planter on the deck or a big pot for this ritual. Each corner of the square needs a candle and a special stone. I get my stones at new-age bookstores, which often have the shiny tumbled versions for as little as a dollar. Mark the corners in a clockwise fashion as follows:

* **Green candle** and peridot or jade for creativity, prosperity, and growth

* **Orange candle** and jasper or onyx for clear thinking and highest consciousness

* **Blue candle** and turquoise or celestine for serenity, kindness, and a happy heart

* **White candle** and quartz or limestone for purification and safety

Greatest Gaia, I turn to you to
help me renew.
Under this new moon and in this
old earth.
Blessings to you; blessings to me.
Blessed be.

Repeat the chant on the left as you light each candle. Put the seeds under the soil with your fingers and tamp them down gently with your wand—the branch—which you should also stick in the ground at this time. Water your new-moon garden and affirmative change will begin in your life that very day.

Basil and Mint Money Bags

Rather than chasing money or possessions, you can simple draw them toward you with wisdom from days gone by. Fill a tiny green pouch with the herbs basil and mint, three cinnamon sticks, one silver dollar (or a shiny pound coin), and a green stone—peridot or a smooth, mossy-colored pebble of jade would be perfect. The untrained eye might perceive this as a bag of weeds and rocks but any kitchen witch recognizes this is a powerful tool for creating dynamic change in your life and attracting good fortune.

Prepare your attraction pouch during a waxing moon; the strongest power would be when the sun or moon are in Taurus, Cancer, or Capricorn. Hold the pouch over frankincense incense and, as the smoke blesses the bag, you speak:

The moon is a silver coin; this I know.
I carry lunar magic with me everywhere I go.
Blessings upon thee and me as my abundance grows.

Carry this power pouch with you as you go about your day—to work, to the store, on your daily walks, to social events. Soon, blessings will shower down upon you. You might even receive a gift or literally find money in your path.

Lucky Seven Almond Attraction Spell

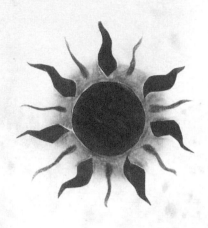

In your pantry, you have much that you need to attract whatever you want more of into your life—love, money, a new home, a new job, increased creativity. The jar of almonds on your shelf is filled with sheer potential, and not just for delicious snacks or dessert. If you are fortunate enough to have an almond tree, harvest your own, but store-bought almonds are just as good. The great psychic Edgar Cayce ate five almonds a day for cancer prevention and believed this healthy nut contained great power. Almond oil is excellent for your skin, applied lightly as a self-blessing. A dab of almond-attraction oil will go far for you, too, in this easy and effective spell.

If you are feeling a financial pinch, try rubbing a dab of almond oil on your wallet and visualize it filling up with money. To engender greater and long-lasting change, perform this spell.

Take seven green votive candles, seven almonds, and seven flat, green leaves from a plant in your garden—ivy or geranium are excellent choices. On your kitchen table, arrange the candles in a circle, placing them on the leaves. Anoint each candle with a dab of almond oil, which works swiftly as it is ruled by Mercury, the god of speed, swift change, and fast communication who operates in the element of Air. Place the almonds in the center. At 7 a.m. or 7 p.m. for seven days, light a candle and eat one almond. Then incant aloud the words on the left.

Luck be quick, luck be kind.
And by lucky seven, good fortune
will be mine.
As above, so below,
The wisdom of the gods shall freely flow.
To perfect possibility, in gratitude I go.

Each day, as the clock strikes seven, perform your ritual. Later, you can count your blessings; there will be at least seven!

Fairy Flora

When planting your garden of enchantments, bear in mind that certain plants attract hummingbirds, butterflies, and fairies. The wee folk love daisies, purple coneflower, French lavender, rosemary, thyme, yarrow, lilac, cosmos, red valerian, sunflowers, honeysuckle, and heliotrope. Folk wisdom handed down through the centuries claims that pansies, blue columbine, and snapdragons planted in a bed are a welcome mat for fairies, and they can use foxglove, which means "folk's glove," to make hats and clothing as well as tulips for their haberdashery. They also favor sunny-faced nasturtiums.

Fairies are quite attached to certain fruit trees with pear, cherry, and apple as their absolute favorites. The hawthorn is one of the most magical trees. It marks the fairies' favorite dancing places and you should not cut or uproot a hawthorn unless you wish to incur their wrath. Keep your eyes peeled when these trees are in bloom as there are bound to be fairy folk about!

103

Very Berry Enchantment Ink

⅛ cup (40ml) crushed berry juice

9 drops of burgundy wine

Dark red ink

Small metal bowl

Apple essential oil

Vial or small, sealable bottle

Paper and envelope

Feather

Red candle

In the days of yore, people often made their own inks, thus imbuing them with a deeply personal energy. They simply went to the side of the road and gathered blackberries from the vines that grew there. Often, a bird flying overhead will supply a gift of volunteer vines, best cultivated by a fence where it can climb, making berry picking easier. When it comes to matters of the heart, contracts, legal letters, and any document of real importance that you feel the need to make your mark upon, an artfully made ink can help you do just that; it can also help you write unforgettable love letters and memorable memorandums. This spell is best performed during the waning moon.

Mix the juice, wine, and red ink in a small, metal bowl. Carefully pour it into the vial and add one drop of the apple essence. Seal the bottle and shake gently.

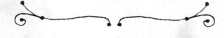

By my hand, this spell is wrought.
With this ink, I will author my own destiny.
And have the happy life and love I sought.
So mote it be.

Incant aloud the spell on the left, and then write the fate you envision for yourself in the near and far future, using the enchantment ink and a feather for a pen. Let it dry and seal it in an envelope and keep on your altar until the new moon phase. Then, by the light of a red candle, open the letter to yourself and read it aloud. Afterward, burn the paper, using the candle, and scatter the ashes in your garden. By the next new moon, you will begin to reap the positive plans you invoked.

Rainwater Renewal Spell

I advise any witchy gardener to have a rain barrel to make the most of stormy weather; you can water your pots of herbs and garden during sunnier days and dry spells. On the first day of the rainfall, place a blue glass bowl outside as a water-catcher. Bring it inside and place on your altar beside a lit candle. Speak these words:

Water of life, gift from the sky,
We bathe in newfound energy, making spirits fly!

Dip your fingers in the water and touch your forehead. Meditate upon the healing work you and your garden can do, thanks to the nurturing rainfall. Pour the water into the ground of your garden, speaking the spell one last time.

GARDEN YOUR WAY TO HAPPINESS

For dispelling negative energy, plant heather, hawthorn, holly, hyacinth, hyssop, ivy, juniper, periwinkle, and nasturtiums.

For healing, plant sage, wort, sorrel, carnation, onion, garlic, peppermint, and rosemary.

Farming and working with plants is guided by the moon and should take place during the waxing moon in the signs of Cancer, Scorpio, Pisces, Capricorn, and Taurus.

Coming Full Circle

"The very act of gardening will be healing. As you continue to practice kitchen witchery, you will learn what works in your spells and which herbs, teas, and plant-based potions and recipes will cause you and your loved ones to flourish."

Chapter 7
Cooking Up
Lots of Love

Magic not only influences desired outcomes, but is empowering and also fosters personal growth. This process is greatly abetted by the carefully crafted love spells and rites of romance in this chapter, which are time-tested, tried, and true. Covering every aspect of amour, you can learn spells that create the potential for love, draw the attention and devotion of a suitor, strengthen the union between a couple, invoke passion, heal after break-up, loss, and divorce, and, perhaps—most importantly—fill your own heart with love and compassion. The romantic repasts and aphrodisiacs are secret recipes shared here for the first time so that you can enjoy them with the one you love. Your affections will be returned threefold with the treasury of charms in this compendium.

Spells to Attract, Create, and Keep Love in Your Life

Like many before me, love spells were my first. At the age of 14, I cast my first, and soon my best friend was the object of amorous attention from a previously disinterested suitor. Since then, I have had many years and ample opportunity to perfect this most joyous aspect of the craft. I have happily watched these spells kindle and keep love's passion alive time and again.

Any metaphysician will tell you the most common requests for help involve matters of the heart. Witchcraft is based in the knowledge that our destinies lie in our own hands, even where love is concerned. Why suffer the slings and arrows of romance gone wrong when you can do something about it? Here are lots of ideas for magical workings so you have a life you love and a life filled with love.

Light of Love: Altar Dedication

Bring love into your life with this altar dedication. Use a small table or chest in your bedroom and cover it with a rich, red scarf or cloth. Adorn it with objects that signify love—red candles, ruby-colored bowls, roses, a statue of Adonis, a heart-shaped chunk of amethyst, whatever stirs your feelings and senses. Give the area a good smudging to purify the space to refresh it for new beginnings. Anoint your candles with oil of jasmine, rose, or any scent that is redolent of romance to you and prepare some similar incense. Light both and speak aloud:

I light the flame,
I fan the flame.
Each candle I burn is a wish,
I desire and will be desired in return.

Twin-Hearts Candle Consecration

If you are seeking a soul mate, this simple spell will do the trick. At nearly any new-age bookshop, you can find heart-shaped, semiprecious stones. On the next new moon, take two pieces of rose quartz and stand in the center of your bedroom. Light two pink candles and recite the words on the right.

Keep the candles and crystals on your bedside table and think of it as shrine to love. Repeat three nights in a row and ready yourself for amour.

Beautiful crystal I hold this night,
Flame with love for my delight.
Harm to none as love comes to me.
This I ask and so shall it be.

Mists of Avalon Potion

3 *drops rose oil*

3 *drops lavender oil*

3 *drops neroli (orange blossom) essence*

½ *cup (120ml) pure distilled water*

If you are dreaming of real romance, you can bring about visions of your future true love with this potent potion.

Pour all the ingredients into a colored-glass spray bottle and shake well three times. Fifteen minutes before you retire, spray lightly on your linens, towel, and pillowcase. Keep a dream journal on your nightstand so you can record details of the great love that will soon manifest.

Flower Charm

Steer me to the highest light;
Guide me to beauty and truth.
Much have I to give.
Much have I to live.
Bright blessings to one and all.

To light the flower of love in your heart, time this charm with the waning of a new Moon. Place a green candle beside a white lily, rose, or freesia. Make sure it is a posy of personal preference. White flowers have the greatest perfume, and any one of these beauties will impart your home with a pleasing aura. I like to float a gardenia in a clear bowl of fresh water, truly the essence of the divine. Light the candle and hold the flower close to your heart. Pray using the spell on the left.

The Art of Spellbinding—Knotted Heartstrings

On a small piece of paper, write the name of the person whose affection you seek in red ink, then roll into a scroll. Anoint the paper with rose oil. Tie the scroll with red thread, speaking one line of the spell on the right per knot.

Keep the scroll on your love altar and burn red candles anointed with rose oil each evening until your will is done. Be very sure of your heart's desire as this spell is everlasting.

One knot to seek my love,
one to find my love.
One to bring my love, one to bind my love.
Forever bound together as one.
So mote it be; this charm is done.

Candied Herbs

The gift of homemade candy is a marvelous way to signal a crush. One of the byproducts of making herbal honey, liqueurs, and oxymels are the candied herbs, which can also be made especially for snacks and for use in sweet-cakes and cookies.

Stir the liquids together in a big pot and heat slowly, stirring every few minutes. Upon reaching boiling point, add the herbs until well mixed. Turn to a slow simmer until the liquid is very thick and sticky. Spoon the herbs out and place on waxed paper to crystallize. Good herbs for this are hyssop, ginger root, lavender, lemon balm, fennel seed, mint, angelica stems, and thyme, as well as small slivers of orange, lime, and lemon.

1 cup (240ml) vodka

1 cup (240ml) simple sugar syrup (see page 66)

1 cup (240ml) honey

2 cups (50g) dried herb of choice

1 large sheet of waxed paper

SLOW COOKERS—FAST RESULTS

Crock-Pots, or slow cookers, became popular in the early 1970s when many women entered the workplace and this humble, helpful appliance could simmer away the evening's supper throughout the day. Along the way, they also became a staple of many pagans' lives, as they are excellent for mulling cider and wine, melting wax for candles, and all manner of crafts and cookery. They are simply the best for soups, stews, and brews, which greatly benefit from the time when flavors can blend together. For candying herbs and the slow work of decoctions, the slow cooker is a marvelous time saver.

Flirty Friday Date-Night Magic

1 cup (240ml) sesame oil

5 drops orange blossom oil

3 drops rose oil

3 drops amber oil

The touch of Venus makes this the most
festive day of the week. This is also the
optimal evening for a tryst! To prepare yourself
for a romantic and flirtatious Friday night, you
must take a goddess bath with the following potion,
stored in a special and beautiful bottle or bowl.

Combine the oils and stir with your fingers six times, silently repeating
three times:

I am a daughter of Venus; I embody love.
My body is a temple of pleasure; I am all that is beautiful.
Tonight, I will drink fully from the cup of love.

Pour two-thirds of this potion into a steaming bath and
meditate upon your evening plans. As you finish,
repeat the Venus spell once more.

Don't use a towel but allow your skin to dry
naturally. Dress up in your finest goddess garb.

Dab a bit of the Venusian oil mix on your pulse points, your
wrists, ankles, and the base of your throat. When you
are out and about this evening, you will most certainly
meet lovely and stimulating new people who are very
interested in you. In fact, they are being drawn to you.

Aphrodite's Ageless Skin Potion

You will notice that many a witch appears ageless. There is a good reason for this; we manifest a lot of joy in our life, including creating potions to take excellent care of our skin for Aphrodite-like youthfulness.

Combine these oils in a sealable, dark-blue bottle. Shake very thoroughly and prepare to anoint your skin with this invocation:

¼ cup (60ml) sweet almond oil (as a base)

2 drops chamomile oil

2 drops rosemary oil

2 drops lavender oil

Goddess of Love, Goddess of Light,
hear this prayer,
Your youth, beauty, and radiance, please share.
So mote it be.

Clean your skin with warm water, then gently daub with the potion. You can also make a salve or balm using my recipe if you want to turn the clock backward. Prepare to be asked for your beauty secrets.

Anointed Lips

The ripest fruit,
The perfect petal,
Each kiss is a spell
of utmost bliss.
And so it is.

From time immemorial, witches have enchanted with their magical beauty. That is because we know how to supplement Mother Nature's gifts. Before a special evening, employ a "kiss of glamour" by adding one drop of clove oil to your favorite pot of lip gloss. While stirring gently, say the words on the left aloud three times.

This will make your lips tingle in a delightful way and give your kisses a touch of spice. The lucky recipient of your affection will be spellbound.

Belles Lettres—RSVP for Romance

Love letters are a very old art that deepen intimacy. What heart doesn't surge when the object of affection pours passion onto a page? Magic ink, prepared paper, and wax will seal the deal. Take a special sheet of paper—sumptuous handmade paper or creamy watermarked fine stationery is ideal—and write with enchanted ink, such as wine-dark dragonsblood, easily found at any metaphysical shop. You can also try the Very Berry recipe in Chapter 6 (see page 104). Perfume the letter with the signature scent or oil your lover prefers, such as amber, vanilla, or ylang-ylang. Seal the letter with a wax, which you have also scented with one precious drop of this oil and, of course, a kiss.

Before your love letter is delivered, light a candle anointed with this oil of love and intone this spell:

Eros, speed my message on wings of desire.
Make my sweetheart burn with love's pure fire.
So mote it be.

Be ready for an ardent answer!

GROW A GARDEN OF EARTHLY DELIGHTS

A happy relationship can be cultivated, literally. By planting and carefully tending plants that have special properties— night-blooming jasmine for heightened sensuality and scent, lilies for lasting commitment, roses for romance—you can nurture your marriage or partnership. During a new moon in the Venus-ruled signs of Taurus or Libra, plant an array of flowers that will enhance mutual devotion.

Gypsy Love Herbs

Many a gypsy woman has enjoyed the fruits of long-lasting love by reciting the following charm while mixing rye and pimento into a dish shared with the object of her affection. While stirring in these amorous herbs, declaim:

Rye of earth, pimento of fire,
Eaten surely lights desire.
Serve to he whose love I crave,
And his heart I will enslave!

Chilled Cucumber Mint Soup For Lovers

3 large, peeled cucumbers
½ cup (15g) fresh mint leaves
1 teaspoon kosher salt
3 tablespoons olive oil

Cucumber has aphrodisiac qualities, according to recent studies, thanks to the veggie's scent. This easy-to-grow delight provides several nutrients essential to maintaining sexual health, including manganese and Vitamins C and K, and it makes for vibrant skin. This is a short and sweet recipe for a refreshingly cold soup to share with a loved one on a hot day.

Put the ingredients in the blender and purée. This gorgeous, green potage makes enough for two servings for a hungry couple. The only accompaniments you need are crispy herb crackers, an icy beverage, and each other.

Be My Valentine: Food Magic

Cucumber is not the only way to set the mood for a night of love. Surprise the object of your affection with one of these treats:

* **Chocolate** is rightly called the "food of the gods."

* **Nutmeg** is held in high regard as an aphrodisiac by Chinese women.

* **Honey**—ever wonder why the time after a wedding is the honeymoon? Bee-sweetened drinks are a must!

* **Oysters** have been celebrated since Roman times for their special aphrodisiac properties.

* **Strawberries** lend a very sweet erotic taste—serve together with chocolate for maximum effect.

* **Vanilla** is little known for its amorous properties, but the taste and scent are powerful.

Sweetheart Shortbread

⅓ cup (10g) candied herbs (see page 111)

⅓ cup (110g) honey

2 sticks (225g) butter, softened

2½ cups (340g) all-purpose (plain) flour

Makes 6

This shortbread makes an excellent gift for a loved one. Cream the herbs and honey into the softened butter and fold the flour into it gradually. Mix well and roll into a 2-inch-wide (5cm) log shape. Wrap this dough in wax paper and chill in the refrigerator for at least 2 hours. Preheat the oven to 325°F/160°C/gas mark 3. Slice rounds of the dough and place onto a greased cookie sheet. Bake for 20 minutes or until the top is beginning to turn golden. Lavender and hyssop make the sweetest dessert shortbreads. Alternatively, omit the honey from the recipe and use sage and thyme for a highly satisfying and savory breakfast shortbread to serve your sweetheart after an exquisite evening.

Aphrodisiac Icing

2 tablespoons water

4 drops vanilla extract

6 lemon balm leaves, plus extra for decorating

2 scant cups (270g) confectioner's (icing) sugar

1 lemon

Candied lemon (using recipe on page 111 for candied herbs)

You can mend broken hearts and enchant any would-be love interest with lemon balm. This recipe takes the cake, either one of your own making or a store-bought spongecake. Glaze the Sweetheart Shortbread above with this icing and you will turn anyone who tastes it into your devotee.

Combine the water, vanilla, and lemon balm and soak overnight. Strain out the herbs and add sugar into the liquid. Grate in zest of the lemon and whisk, squeezing in some lemon juice if needed for liquid consistency. Pour this icing over the cake and top with candied lemon and balm. This distinctive dessert is a spell spun of sugar.

Crushing on Coffee

6 cardamom pods

1 cinnamon stick

½ cup (110g) ground coffee beans

6 cups (1.5 liters) water

Cream or another type of creamer (e.g. Half & Half)

1 tablespoon honey or raw sugar

Cardamom is a spice the Indians, creators of the Kama Sutra, used to good effect. Called the "grains of paradise," you can find it in any grocery and recognize the organic kind by the green color of the pods.

Crush the cardamom pods with a pestle and mortar and extract the seeds, discarding the pods. Break the cinnamon into pieces and grind together with the cardamom seeds and stir into the ground coffee. Make coffee as you usually would, using a French press or coffee maker for four cups brimming with bliss. The strong, rich flavor does call for cream and sweetening, so you quite literally sweeten the pot and serve it up for an amorous and energetic evening.

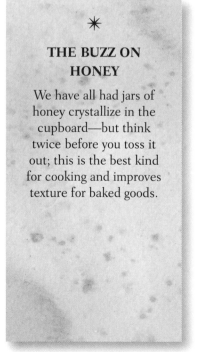

*

THE BUZZ ON HONEY

We have all had jars of honey crystallize in the cupboard—but think twice before you toss it out; this is the best kind for cooking and improves texture for baked goods.

Lover's Tea

Here is a quick recipe to create exactly the right mood for a dreamy evening.

Stir all the ingredients together in a clockwise motion. You can store this in a tin or colored jar for up to a year for those special evenings. When you are ready to brew the tea, pour boiling water over the herbs, two teaspoons for a cup of water. Say the following spell aloud during the 5-minute steeping and picture your heart's desire.

1 ounce (28g) dried hibiscus flowers

1 ounce (28g) dried and pulverized rosehips

½ ounce (14g) peppermint

½ ounce (14g) dried lemon balm

Herbal brew of love's emotion
With my wish I fortify
When two people share this potion
This love shall intensify
As in the Olde Garden of Love.

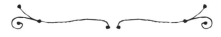

Sweeten to taste with honey and share this luscious libation with the one you love.

Coming Full Circle

"At the end of life, all that matters is how much love you gave to the world, how much of your heart you shared with people."

Chapter 8

Celebrating the Wheel of the Year

The human heart longs for ritual and ways to mark life passages. The pagan calendar handles that wonderfully by reminding us of the cycles of nature and the importance of spending time in community. Nearly all our modern high holidays have ancient roots in farming customs and fertility rituals to ensure good crops and plenty for all. Lunar moon festivals, solstice seasonal galas, and major sabbat celebrations call for ceremonial magic, family feasts, and acknowledgment of the natural world. This is the time to count our blessings and share them. Observing these high holy days with the circle rites, magical foods, and pagan prayers herein assures that your kitchen will be a temple dedicated to joy for many years to come.

Mystical Meals
and Holiday Rituals

Sabbats are the holy days for each season of the year, in accordance with the celestial spheres above. Some of these holy days celebrate the arrival of spring and the start of new growth, while others mark the harvest in preparation for the dark and chilly days of winter. Nearly all our festivals have roots in the ancient rites based in fertility and the hopes of abundant farm crops. Humankind first marked time by the movement of the stars, Sun, and Moon in the sky, which also informed the designation of constellations and astrological calendars. Candlemas, Beltane, Lammas Day, and All Hallow's Eve are the major sabbats. The lesser sabbats, listed below, are the astrological markers of new seasons:

* **Ostara:** March 21, also known as the Vernal or Spring Equinox

* **Litha:** June 21, commonly known as the Summer Solstice

* **Mabon:** September 21, best known as the Autumnal Equinox

* **Yule:** December 21, is the Winter Solstice

Candlemas—The Coming Season

Candlemas, on February 2, also known as Imbolc, is the highest point between the winter solstice and spring equinox. This festival anticipates the coming of spring with banquets and blessings. Tradition holds that milk must be served and modern pagans have expanded that to butter cookies, ice cream, and cheeses; and any other related food should be shared. It is an important time to welcome new members of your spiritual circle and new witches into a coven. Candlemas is a heartwarming occasion, but it is still a wintry time so kindling for the hearth or bonfire should include cedar, pine, juniper, and holly along with wreaths of the same to mark the four cardinal points, alongside white candles in glass votives. Strong incense such as cedar, nag champa, or frankincense will bless the space. The circle leader shall begin the ritual by lighting incense from the fire and, facing each direction, and saying:

Welcome Guardians of the East, bringing your fresh winds and
breath of life. Come to the circle of Imbolc.
Welcome Guardians of the South, you bring us heart and health.
Come to the circle on this holy day.
Welcome Guardians of the West, place of setting sun and mighty
mountains. Come to us.
Welcome Guardians of the North, land of life-giving rains and
snow. Come to our circle on this sacred day.

The leader should welcome each member of the circle and speak of the gifts they bring to the community. Everyone should acknowledge one another with toasts and blessings and break bread together in this time of the coming season.

Cakes and Ale—Saturn-Day Night Fever

Here is a pagan party plan, which is wonderful for weekend evenings. You can add many embellishments, such as important astrological or lunar happenings, but you should gather your friends or coven and celebrate life any Saturday night of your choosing. If the weather is warm enough, have the festivities outside. Otherwise, make sure to choose an indoor space with enough room for dancing, drumming, and major merriment. Ask each of your guests to bring cake, cookies, and candies of their choice along with their favorite beer, wine, mead, cider, or ale, and sitting cushions. Place the offerings on a center-table altar and light candles of all colors. Once everyone is seated and settled, the host or designated circle leader chants:

Gods of Nature, bless these cakes.
That we may never suffer hunger.
Goddess of the harvest,
Bless this ale,
That we may never suffer thirst. Blessed be.

The eldest and the youngest should serve the food and drink to all in the circle. Lastly, they serve each other and the leader chants the blessing again. Let the feasting begin!

Spiritual Spring Cleaning: the Bean Blessing

The change of season at the Vernal Equinox, on March 21, brings about the need for new energies, which you can engender with cleansing. Here is an ancient way to cast out "the old" and bring in glad tidings and positive new beginnings for your friends and family.

Grab a bag of beans from your kitchen and invite your circle over. In ancient times, many pagan peoples, from Incans to Egyptians and Greeks, believed beans contained evil spirits, so this rite comes from that lineage. Go to your roof or the highest point of your house which you can get to safely and give everyone a handful of beans. Each person throws one bean at a time, calling out whatever they need to bid goodbye to—a bad habit, nightmare job, whatever your personal demons may be. After everyone has tossed the negativity and discord away, celebrate the clean slate. Fun note, if you toss lentils into a barren field in the spring, by fall, you will be able to harvest enough for many pots of soup!

✳

SPROUT INTO SPRING
ALL YEAR-ROUND

Sprouts are immensely nutritious and fairly effortless to grow: add one teaspoon of seeds to a quart jar filled with water and cover with cheesecloth. After 24 hours, turn the jar upside down and drain. After at least 2 hours, refill and repeat this process twice a day for 3–5 days. You'll have a rich repast for salads, sandwiches, soups, and stir fries. Try these seeds for endless healthy options: sunflower, mung bean, broccoli, quinoa, lentil, radish, mustard, alfalfa, red clover, and fenugreek.

Beltane Eve

Beltane, celebrated on April 30, is without doubt the sexiest of pagan high holidays, and it is anticipated greatly throughout the year. Witchy ones celebrate this holy night, and it is traditional for celebrations to last all through the night. This is a festival for feasting, singing, laughter, and lovemaking. On May Day, when the sun returns in the morning, revelers gather to erect a merrily beribboned Maypole to dance around, followed by picnics and sensual siestas. The recipe below is befitting this special time of the year when love flows as freely as wine.

Beltane Brew

1 quart (1 liter) honey

3 quarts (3 liters) distilled water

Herbs to flavor, such as cinnamon, nutmeg, vanilla, according to your preference

1 packet (7g) of active dry yeast

Honeyed mead is revered as the drink of choice for this sexiest of pagan holy days. It is an aphrodisiac and signals the ripeness of this day devoted to love and lust. This recipe is adapted from a medieval method.

Mix the honey and water. Boil for 5 minutes. You can add the herbs to your liking but I prefer a tablespoon each of clove, nutmeg, cinnamon, and allspice. Add a packet of yeast and mix. Put everything in a large container. Cover with plastic wrap and allow to rise and expand. Store the mix in a dark place and allow it to set for seven days, ideally at the beginning of a new-moon phase. Refrigerate for three days while the sediment settles at the bottom. Strain and store in a colored glass bottle, preferably green. You can drink it now but after seven months, it will have gained a full-bodied flavor. Always keep in a cool dark place.

Nonalcoholic Mead

Boil all the mixed ingredients for five minutes and let cool. Bottle immediately in a colored glass jar. Keep this in the fridge to avoid fermentation and enjoy during any festive occasion. This is a healthy and refreshing way to celebrate.

1 quart (1 liter) honey
3 quarts (3 liters) distilled water
½ cup (120ml) lemon juice
1 lemon, sliced
½ teaspoon nutmeg
pinch of salt

Hoof and Horn Rite

Ideally, you would celebrate outdoors, but if indoor-bound on Beltane Eve, pick a place with a fireplace and have a roaring blaze, so celebrants can wear comfy clothing and dance barefoot. Ask them to bring spring flowers and musical instruments, plenty of drums! Place pillows on the floor and serve an ambrosial spread of finger foods, honeyed mead, beer, spiced cider, wine, and fruity teas. As you light circle incense, set out green, red, and white candles, one for each participant. When it is time to call the circle, raise your arm and point to each direction, saying "To the east, to the north," etc., then sing:

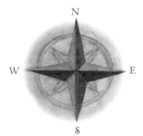

Hoof and horn, hoof and horn, tonight our
spirits are reborn [repeat thrice]
Welcome, joy, to this home. Fill these friends
with love and laughter. So mote it be.

Have each guest light a candle and speak to the subject of love with a toast of Beltane Brew. Drumming and dancing is the next part of the circle. This is truly an invocation of lust for life and will be a night to remember for all. Now rejoice!

Sacred Grove Solstice Spell

Celebrating the season of the sun, on June 21, is best done outdoors in the glory of nature's full bloom. If you have a forest nearby or a favorite grove of trees, plan to picnic and share this rite of passage with your spiritual circle. Covens often have a favorite spot. All the better if a great oak is growing there, the tree most sacred to druids. Gather the tribe and bring brightly colored ribbons and indelible markers. Form the circle by holding hands, then point to east, south, north, and west, chanting:

We hold the wisdom of the sun,
We see the beauty of our earth.
To the universe that gives us life, we return the gift.
Deepest peace to all,
And we are all one. Blessed be.

Each member of the circle should speak their wish for the world, themselves, or loved ones and write it on a ribbon. One by one, tie your ribbon to a tree. Each flutter of the wind will spread your well wishes.

Summer Solstice Pudding

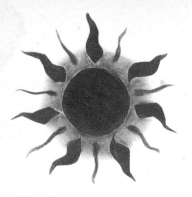

Inspired by a traditional recipe from Kent, known as "The Garden of England," this summer pudding brings forth the taste of the season, simply sublime.

Combine all the fruit and sugar in a saucepan and gently boil for 3 minutes. Squeeze in the juice of half a lemon. Line a big bowl with the bread, overlapping to form a crust. Pour in the fruit mix. Add one last bread slice to cover the mixture and place a saucer on top with a weight on it to press down. Cover with plastic wrap and chill in the refrigerator overnight. Before serving, turn the dish upside down and the pudding will slip out in a half-circle shape. Top with fresh whipped cream and a few berries and mint leaves as garnish. This cool treat could not be easier. Each spoonful is filled with the sweetness of summer.

1 pound (450g) fresh mixed berries—strawberries, raspberries, blueberries, blackberries

1 cup (225g) diced fresh peaches, plums, nectarines

¼ cup (50g) sugar

juice of ½ lemon

10 slices crust-less bread (or 15 biscuits or shortbreads)

Lammas Day—Harvesting Happiness

This major sabbat, on August 2, denotes the high point of the year; the crops are in their fullness, the weather is warm, and the countryside is bursting forth with the beauty of life. Pagans know we have the heavens above to thank for this and the gods of nature must be acknowledged for their generosity with a gathering of the tribe and a feast, ideally in the great outdoors.

Ask invitees to bring harvest-themed offerings for the altar: gourds, pumpkins, bundles of wheat stalks and corn, fresh pickings from their garden, and food to share in thanksgiving made from the same—pies, tomato salads, cucumber pickles, green beans, corn pudding, watermelon, lemon cakes, apple cider, and beer brewed from wheat, hops, and barley. This celebration of the harvests of the summer season should reflect what you have grown with your own hands. Fill your cauldron or a big, beautiful colored glass bowl half-full with freshly drawn water and get packets of tiny votive candles to float in it. At the feast table, make sure to have a place setting for the godly guest Lugh, who watched over the plantings to ensure this bounty. Place loaves of Lammas bread by his plate.

When all guests have arrived, everyone should add a food offering to the plate of the god and light a candle to float in the cauldron. Cut a slice of Lammas bread for Lugh and begin the ceremony with this prayer of thanks:

Oh, ancient Lugh of the fields and farms,
We invite you here with open arms,
In this place between worlds, in flowering fields of hay.
You have brought the blessings we receive this Lammas Day.

Begin the feast and, before the dessert course, everyone should go around the table and speak of their gratitude for the gifts of the year. Storytelling, singing, spiral dances, and all manner of merriment are part of Lammas Day.

Lugh Lore—Guardian of the Harvest

The "Shining One" from the Celtic mythology, Lugh is the warrior sun god and also guardian of crops. The Lughnassa is a festival in honor of the harvest god, taking place at the beginning of every August. Lammas, which means "loaf mass," was the Anglo Saxon's fete for the first harvest of the year and included sport competitions in addition to feasting, dancing, and ritual. The Scottish caber toss, a log-throwing contest, derives from this sort of yearly folk Olympics. These two early-August festivals were conflated over the centuries, with Lammas becoming ingrained in the pagan calendar.

At the end of summer and fall, kitchen witches should hold rituals of gratitude for the abundance of the crops and for the gift that is life. This will keep the flow of prosperity coming to you and yours. Lugh also has domain over late-summer storms, so anyone experiencing drought or wildfires can pray to Lugh for rains to come.

Lammas Day Bread

This recipe makes 1 large or 2 regular loaves.

Mix the dry ingredients in a large bowl. Add the peanut butter and honey to the hot milk and stir to combine. Cool the milk mixture to warm and pour into the dry ingredients. Knead for 15 minutes, adding the extra flour, if needed, to make a smooth and elastic dough. Oil the surface of the dough, cover with plastic wrap or a damp kitchen towel, and let rise in a warm place until it has doubled in size; this usually takes 90 minutes. Punch it down and shape into your desired loaf size. Allow to rise again, covered in a warm place.

Bake in a preheated oven at 375°F/190°C/gas mark 5 for 30 minutes until golden brown and hollow-sounding when you rap on the bottom.

2 cups (270g) whole-wheat flour, plus an additional ½ cup (70g) set aside

2 cups (270g) bread flour

¼ cup (35g) toasted sesame seeds

2 tablespoons active dry yeast

2½ teaspoons salt

2 tablespoons peanut butter

2 tablespoons honey

2 cups (475ml) milk, scalded

Fall Equinox Festival—Mabon

Your kitchen is not just where you prepare meals, concoct healing tonics, and craft enchantments; it is also a temple with an altar where you honor spirit. This change-of-seasons sabbat of Mabon, on September 21, marks the turning of weather and the other face of nature. Mark the four directions on your altar with a loaf of bread in the east, a bowl of apples in the south, a bottle of wine in west, and an ear of Indian corn in the north.

✳

LEAFY LEGEND—
GRABBING LUCK BY THE HAND

Here is a sweet bit of alchemy available to all, handed down from medieval times. Wise women of yore taught their children to look for falling leaves. To catch one in your hand is the best kind of luck, directly from Mother Nature herself. Carry it with you for a season and you will be safe from harm and find gifts in your path. If you are especially blessed to catch two leaves in one season, the second is for your companion of destiny. You will be bound by both feeling and fortune.

Corn Moon Clan Pot

Here we have the best of both worlds in one pot. Kids will love this "a-maize-ing" dish—they will ask for seconds!

In a large pan over high heat, combine the pasta, tomatoes, enchilada sauce, and water. Heat to a boil, then reduce the temperature to medium heat; add the chicken, black beans, corn, and salsa. If your family likes it extra hot, throw in some green peppers to turn the heat up a notch. Reduce the heat to low, cover, and let simmer for 20 minutes, or until the pasta is tender and cooked through. Top with the cheese and the herbs; place the lid on the pan. Let the cheese melt in for 5 minutes and serve up this global crowd pleaser in heaping bowls.

It can be a nice meal to serve during the Corn Moon and ritual feasts involving growth and transformation. Corn is associated with self-sustainability and fecundity, both of people and of the land. Sharing this dish on the September full Moon is a time to remember and be grateful for all we have sown and all we have reaped to acknowledge the continuing cycles of life.

2 cups (200g) dry penne pasta

8 ounces (225g) diced tomatoes

1 jar enchilada sauce, 8 ounces (225g)

1½ cups (350ml) water

2 cups (250g) shredded, cooked chicken

1 can black beans

1 cup (175g) fresh (or frozen) corn

2 tablespoons salsa

2 tablespoons hot sauce

½ cup (50g) Cheddar cheese, grated

Basil, cilantro (coriander), chives, avocado, and sour cream

Samhain—All Hallows' Eve

Halloween, on October 31, stems from the grand tradition of the Celtic New Year. What started as a folk festival celebrated by small groups in rural areas has come to be the second largest holiday nowadays in North America and is increasingly gaining popularity in the UK and the rest of Europe. There are multitudinous reasons, including modern marketing, but I think it satisfies a basic human need to let your "wild side" out, to be free and more connected with the ancient ways. This is the time when the veil between worlds is thinnest and you can commune with the other side, with elders, and the spirit world. It is important to honor the ancestors during this major sabbat and acknowledge what transpired in the passing year as well as set intentions for the coming one.

This is the ideal time to invite your circle; the ideal number for your "coven" is 13. Gather powdered incense, salt, a loaf of bread, goblets for wine, and three candles to represent the triple goddess for altar offerings. Ideally on an outdoor stone altar, pour the powdered incense into a pentagram star shape. Let go of old sorrows, angers, and anything not befitting new beginnings in this new year. Bring only your best to this auspicious occasion.

Light the candles and say:

In honor of the Triple
Goddess on this sacred
night of Samhain,
All the ancient ones,
From time before time,
To those behind the veil.

A DIFFERENT KIND OF CANDLE MAGIC

Drips, drops, and spills of candle wax come with the territory of witchery. Scraping doesn't work and leaves a bigger mess. Here's the trick: take a damp terrycloth towel and place over the wax spill; put a hot iron on it for a minute and the wax will be pulled up into the cloth. Abracadabra: the wax has vanished.

Rap the altar three times and light the incense. Say this blessing aloud:

> For this bread, wine, and salt,
> We ask the blessings of Mother,
> Maiden, and Crone,
> And the gods who guard the
> Gate of the World.

Sprinkle salt over the bread, eat the bread, and drink the wine.

Each of the celebrants should come to the altar repeating the bread and wine blessing. After this, be seated and everyone in turn should name those on the other side and offer thanks to ancestors and deities. This can and should take a long time as we owe much to loved ones on the other side.

New Year's Kitchen

A form of magic handed down from antiquity is to have a domestic goddess figure in your home; archaeologists have found them amongst the most ancient artifacts. It is a good energy generator to have such a figurine decorating your kitchen altar. The most important consideration is to choose the divinity with which you feel the deepest connection.

Salt Dough Deity Recipe

A marvelous group ritual to hold is a "kitchen warming." Invite over a group of friends and bake up a batch of goddesses from this list or your own inspiration. Salt dough is used to create lovely domestic sculptures, such as braided breads that are lacquered to decorate your domicile. This easy and fun approach will bless your homes for the seasons to come. You can double or triple the amounts based on how many goddesses are working together.

2 cups (270g) flour
1 cup (200g) salt
½ cup (120ml) water

Mix the three ingredients together and then knead gently by hand, adding in teaspoons of additional water until the dough is completely smooth. Rest on a clean, dry wooden chopping board for half an hour. If you want to have colored dough, add in an organic food coloring, which you drop into the water at the beginning. Blue, green, yellow, red, orange, and purple are perfect to represent goddesses.

Shape your goddess as you see fit or use an image from a book that speaks to you. Once your goddess is sculpted, place her in the oven at a low temperature of 250°F/120°C/gas mark ½ and bake for at least 2 hours until the surface is firm to the touch. Take her out and let her cool, then decorate with paint, glitter, beads, jewels, and all the ornamentation suitable to her royal station.

I love the apple tree in my back yard. To honor the fruit goddess Pomona, I shape a simple image of her with an apple-wreath crown, painted red and green. When spring rains bring apple blossoms, I return Pomona to the tree over which she watches. Each year, there are more apples thanks to her generosity.

✳

NUTTY BUT GENIUS

Before you have your circle over for festivities, you need to prepare the temple, your home. The humble walnut was sacred to King Solomon and grew in the Hanging Gardens of Babylon. Head to the pantry for this penny-wise preparation: you can remove marks from wooden furniture by halving a walnut and rubbing the edge along the grain of the wood. House magic!

Global Goddesses Every Kitchen Witch Should Know

* **Chicomecoatl:** this Aztec corn goddess brings prosperity to farmers

* **Dugnai:** this Slavic deity is a house guardian and blesser of breads

* **Fornax:** here is the goddess of all ovens, Roman in origin; she guards against hunger

* **Frigg:** this benevolent Nordic being watches over the domestic arts (including love)

* **Fuchi:** the Japanese invoke her when they need fires—cooking fire, campfire, and celebrations

* **Hebe:** daughter of Hera and Zeus, this goddess of youth is also a cupbearer who can bless your chalices and kitchen ritual vessels

* **Hehsui-no-kami:** in Japan, she is the kitchen goddess and she can be yours, too

* **Huixtocihuatl:** the Aztec goddess of salt is one to turn to and thank each and every day

* **Ida:** the subcontinent of India looks to her who rules fire and spiritual devotion

* **Ivenopae:** the Indonesian mother of rice helps at harvest time, feeding millions

* **Li:** nourishing fires is the charge of this Chinese goddess

* **Nikkai:** the first fruits of the season are the gifts of this Canaanite holiness

* **Ogetsu-hime:** this dependable deity is the Japanese goddess of food

* **Okitsu-hime:** revered from ancient times is this Japanese kitchen goddess

* **Pirua:** Peru's mother of maize is sacred to all who rely on her for survival

* **Pomona:** the fruit goddess of Roman times has domain over gardens and orchards

* **Saule:** this Baltic benefic is a sun goddess who lights the hearth fires and all homely arts

Yule—Winter Solstice Bonfire

December is named for the Roman goddess Decima, one of the three fates. The word "yule" comes from the Old Norse *jol*, which means midwinter and is celebrated on the shortest day of the year, December 21. The old tradition was to have a vigil at a bonfire to make sure the sun did indeed rise again. This primeval custom evolved to become a storytelling evening and while it may well be too cold to sit outside in snow and sleet, congregating around a blazing hearthfire, dining, and talking deep into the night are still important for your community truly to know one another, impart wisdom, and speak of hopes and dreams. Greet the new sun with stronger connections and a shared vision for the coming solar year.

WINTER-IS-COMING ROOT ROAST

We live in a time when some of the very foods the early Yule celebrants feasted upon are having a renaissance—bone broths, root vegetables, and stone fruits. These are simple to prepare and share with the clan. The following root veggies are magnificent when roasted with rosemary for 40 minutes at 450°F/230°C/gas mark 8 with a drizzling of olive oil and salt: 2 pounds (1kg) mix-and-match medium-sized yams, potatoes, garlic, mushrooms, onions, parsnips, carrots, and beets. In the rare chance of leftovers, these can become the basis for a heart-warming soup or stew.

Coming Full Circle
"This path is not only about looking inward, but also about becoming attuned to the world around you—every leaf, stone, blade, flower, and seed; the highest calling of any pagan is to achieve harmony with the cycles of the natural world."

Conclusion:

Journaling Your Spellcraft

The art and practice of kitchen witchery is, at the core, an expression of your spirituality. While many of the sabbat celebrations and circle rites are gatherings of the tribe, much of your spellcraft will be performed by a coven of one—you. And it is the "inner work" of devising and creating personal rituals, tracking life cycles of the moon and stars, and recording your magical workings in your Book of Shadows that will encourage your deepest spiritual development. Your life is a work in progress and here is a record of it. The insights you gain from going back and considering all that has come before are priceless. Here should be your musings, your invocations, hopes, and intentions. I call this the Journal of the Journey and it can take any form your imagination conjures, as long as the deep truths and revelations of your work are captured.

These next few pages of prompts are all for you to record your magical musings and inspired ideas. Keep these and look back now and again for reflection. You may discover that the entries penned in this journal were the first steps in renewal and new directions in your life. This record of your own wisdom is a priceless treasure.

Blessed be from my kitchen to yours!

The new-Moon phase is the time for fresh ventures, renewing, cleansing, and clearing. What seeds will you sow during this time for new beginnings?

A waxing moon is the time for abundance, attraction, and love magic. It can also heal rifts and protect existing relationships. What do you want to attract during this time?

The full Moon shines a light on challenges in your life; now is the time to release and let go of anything causing problems. What are the issues or old patterns you should "catch and release"?

....

....

....

....

....

....

....

....

The waning moon is a time to emphasize the positive by banishing the negative. Rid yourself of any unconstructive feelings, habits, health challenges, or thoughts; clear out the psychic clutter with the spells you have learned and replace it with good energy. What psychic clutter do you need to clear?

....

....

....

....

....

....

....

....

....

....

Circles and group rituals often occur only on high holy days. What is some of the solo spellwork you want to explore during the rest of the year? What rituals would you like to design and create?

....

....

....

....

....

....

....

Intention-setting is one of the most powerful ways through which you can bring positive change into your life. It is a vital kind of inner-work. What are your magical intentions and visions for the days and weeks to come?

....

....

....

....

....

....

....

....

....

As your garden grows, so does your wisdom and well-being. Which plants, potions, herbs, and flowers function best in your magical workings? Which would you like to add for the next spring?

....
....
....
....
....
....
....
....
....

Your home is your sanctuary. As a kitchen witch and practitioner of house magic, how can you create a more peaceful, beautiful, healthy, and happy domicile for yourself and your loved ones?

....
....
....
....
....
....
....
....
....

Index

Acknowledgments

I have much to be thankful for in my life and I count among
my blessings the CICO "Dream Team." I have been writing and
publishing for several years and I have never experienced such
a plentitude of grace and good work. Kudos to publisher Cindy
Richards for this examplar in the world of book publishing. I am
grateful to in-house editor Carmel Edmonds for polishing this
book into a jewel and for Jennifer Jahn's eagle-eyed copyediting.
Emma Garner's luscious illustrations are simply delightful and,
along with Emily Breen's expert design, they bring the pages to
life. Heaps of gratitude to the one-and-only Kristine Pidkameny
who guided this project from idea to reality and made it fun in the
process. I am inspired by all of you!